Bali and Beyond

Other books by Colin Simpson

THE NEW AUSTRALIA
GREECE: The Unclouded Eye
KATMANDU
THE VIKING CIRCLE
(Denmark, Norway, Sweden, Finland, Iceland, Greenland)
TAKE ME TO RUSSIA (U.K. ed.: *This is Russia*)
TAKE ME TO SPAIN
WAKE UP IN EUROPE
THE COUNTRY UPSTAIRS
(U.K. ed.: *Picture of Japan;* U.S. ed.: *Japan, An Intimate View*)
ASIA'S BRIGHT BALCONIES *(Hong Kong: Macao: Philippines)*
ADAM IN OCHRE *(Inside Aboriginal Australia)*
ADAM WITH ARROWS *(Inside New Guinea)*
ADAM IN PLUMES *(New Guinea)*
ISLANDS OF MEN *(Inside Melanesia)*
PLUMES AND ARROWS *(Inside New Guinea, a combination)*
SHOW ME A MOUNTAIN *(the Ampol story)*
COME AWAY PEARLER *(a novel)*

COLIN SIMPSON

Bali
and Beyond

ANGUS AND ROBERTSON

First published in 1972 by

ANGUS AND ROBERTSON (PUBLISHERS) PTY LTD
102 Glover Street, Cremorne, Sydney
2 Fisher Street, London
107 Elizabeth Street, Melbourne
167 Queen Street, Brisbane
89 Anson Road, Singapore

© *Colin Simpson 1972*

National Library of Australia
card number and ISBN 0 207 12503 1

Registered in Australia for transmission by post as a book
PRINTED IN AUSTRALIA BY WATSON FERGUSON AND CO. BRISBANE

Contents

Illustrations

Bali

Miles Scale: 0 5 10 15 20 25 30

Author's Route

(Mountain heights in feet)

▲ 1030

▲ 1410

▲ 3300

G. Merbuk 4550

▲ 4260

▲ 4050

▲ G. Patas 4650

▲ 3320

JAVA

BALI STRAIT

GILIMANUK

NEGARA

Pulukan

Tjelukanbawang

Bubunan

L. Tamblin

Indonesia

MALAYSIA (West)

MALAYSIA (East)

SINGAPORE

SUMATRA

KALIMANTAN (Borneo)

SULAWESI (Celebes)

HALMAHERA

Moluccas

WEST IRIAN (New Guinea)

Djakarta

JAVA

BALI

SUMBA

SUMBAWA

KOMODO

FLORES

CERAM

BANDA

TIMOR

Darwin

AUSTRALIA

Miles Scale: 0 500 1000 1500

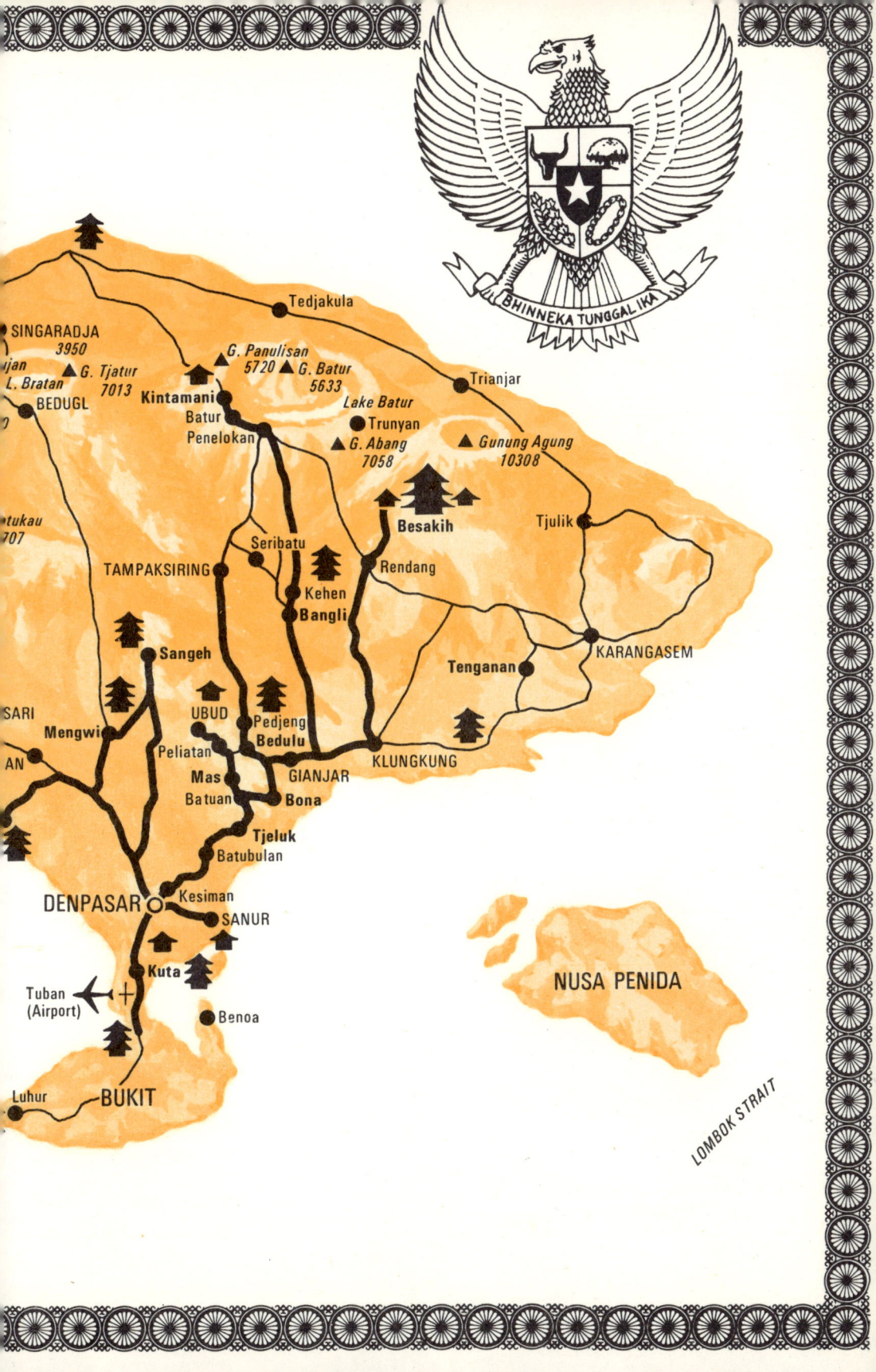

Bali

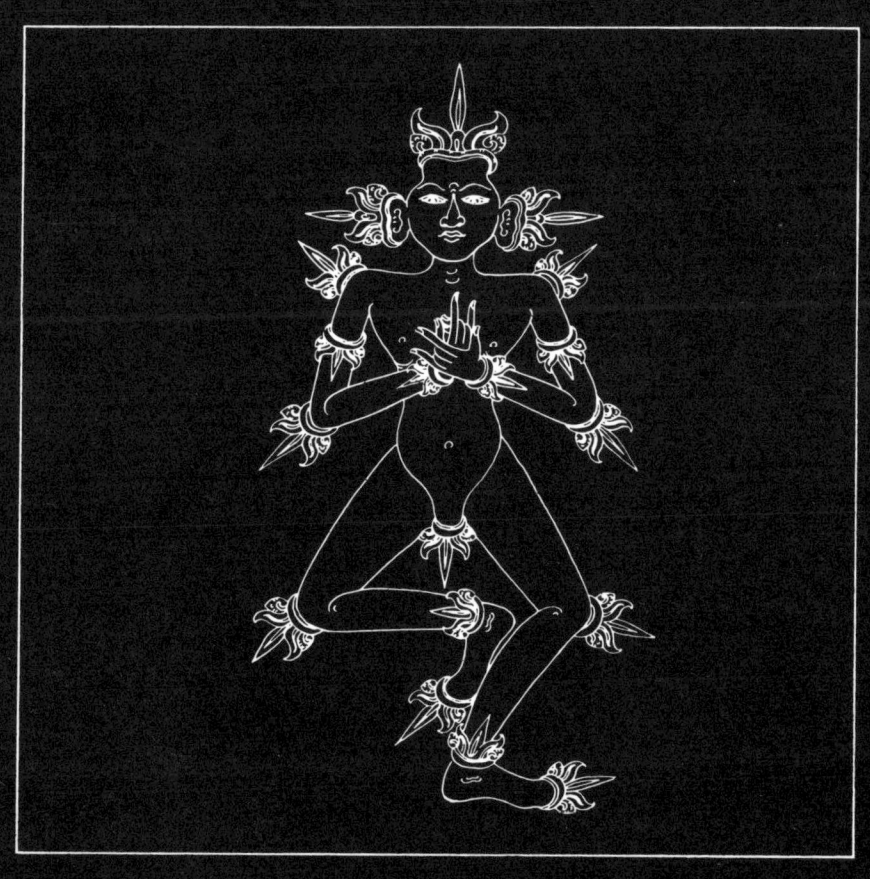

Tourists haven't spoilt it

"CHAMPAGNE, sir, or orange juice?" the Garuda airline hostess asked. The man sitting next to me creased a bland Dutch face with a smile and said, "Both."

They mixed quite well, the Dutchman said, as the Javanese girl with a skin like smoked honey poured Moët into half a glass of orange juice that looked pale yellow beside the vivid saffron of her uniform. I said I'd try this rich man's orangeade.

It tasted right enough for a time of day when I normally wouldn't drink anything, eleven thirty in the morning. We were sitting in first class in a DC 8 on the tarmac at Sydney airport. Remembering airlines that have you in the sky for half an hour before they can produce a drink of any kind, I chalked up a good-cabin-service mark for Garuda Indonesian Airways. (Garuda is the name of an eagle that flies in Hindu mythology with the god Vishnu on its back.) The aircraft was waiting for Control to clear its take-off for Bali and points west to Amsterdam.

We took off. When the captain spoke he said the direct flight to Bali would take six hours. I was getting off at Bali.

"Bali." The Dutchman pronounced the *a* broad, as the English and Australians do, not narrowing it as the Americans do so that it rhymes with *valley*. "I was once there."

He was there when all that is now Indonesia was Dutch East Indies, and Java (which he pronounced Yaava) he had known

1

much better than Bali. He felt that Bali would not be so good now. Too many tourists. The champagne of international tourism could not be poured into the orange juice of the Balinese way of life. The two wouldn't mix. So the Dutchman said.

He wasn't saying a thing that I hadn't read in half a dozen places. About how influx of tourists would spoil Bali, corrode the Balinese lifestyle, debase the island's arts, cloud its mirror with materialism. Tourism, the soothsayers said, would filch away Bali's natural happiness at the same time as it put money in Balinese pockets. Nobody said that this despoilation of Bali had actually set in. Only that, as sure as sunset, it would come about in the future as the tourist trade grew.

The tourist trade had already grown. Leapt, in fact, since the opening of the international airport in 1969, which began the boom of the Bali Beach Inter-Continental Hotel. In 1970 Bali got 40,000 tourists, and more in 1971.

Some of the forebodings were already sounding funny. Like the American museum man Philip Hanson Hiss saying in his book *Bali*,[1] written in 1940, that one good thing the Second World War would do was halt the tourist trade to Bali. "Perhaps it has delayed for a year, or even a decade, the fateful dissolution of Balinese culture."

BALINESE CULTURE is the flower of the bulb that is Balinese religion. This bulb no longer grows in any other part of the Indonesian garden. Religiously, Bali is the nation's last active temple of Hinduism: the rest is predominantly Moslem. Had Islamic conquest brought the Balinese into the mosque, or the missionaries of Dutch colonialism got them into the Christian church, that would have been the end of the Balinese culture that Westerners found surviving in this century and fell in love with.

Hardy survivor though it had shown itself to be, the traditional Balinese lifestyle was not necessarily indestructible. But that it should crumble as a result of tourist visitation seemed to me about as likely as that the Basilica of St Peter in Rome would. Indeed, tourism would be cooking its own gold-egg-laying goose to the extent that it caused any dissolution of the culture the tourists came flying in to see.

2

Tourism is not change's prime instrument. Education is. So, the romantic who wants to preserve the Balinese lifestyle by blowing up the Hotel Bali Beach is guying the wrong Fawkes. He will get nowhere unless he essays the daunting task of putting a firestick to the primary school that is now in nearly every Balinese village—and he had best reserve his explosives for the university at Denpasar, the capital.

The Communists well knew the uses of education for indoctrination. It was the PKI (Partei Kommunista Indonesia, with which President Sukarno was hand in glove) that posed the threat of threats to traditional Bali. About eight hundred of Bali's two thousand schoolteachers were Communists or sympathizers. They sought to weaken the religion at the same time as they advocated a more equitable deal for the eighty per cent of Balinese farmers who don't own the ricelands they cultivate so picturesquely. By 1965, jargon would say, a great deal of divisiveness had been activated among the Balinese people—the people Hiss had described twenty-five years earlier as "the happiest people in the world".[1]

When the Communist Party in September 1965 murdered six of the Army's top generals in Djakarta, and still failed to seize power, anti-Communist pogroms swept Indonesia. The Balinese of whom Hiss wrote, "It is an inspiration to know that man can live at peace and harmony with man",[1] killed their fellow men to the number of approximately 40,000. Look at Bali and it seems incredible that such a massacre could happen there, in this "paradise" of the tourist brochures.

CHANGES there have been, of course, since Bali was first made widely known to the West in the thirties, through photographs and such books as the notable *Island of Bali*[2] by the Mexican artist Miguel Covarrubias. The photographs of Balinese beauties soon had the comedians saying that any man who went to Bali could expect "a good bust in the eye". Bare-bosomed comeliness was the island's trademark attraction.

Yet even in 1933 Balinese women in Denpasar, the principal town, had "taken to wearing clumsy blouses",[3] clumsy in the sense that they were blouses of the *badju* (Malay) style—which women in North Bali had been wearing since 1882. when they

3

were ordered by the Dutch authorities to cover their breasts so that the Dutch soldiery would not be inflamed. South Bali—which is today the tourists' Bali—was only nominally under Dutch rule until 1906.

Some people blame the cover-up on tourism and say that · lovely young Balinese women were embarrassed into blouses by being stared at and stalked by drooling camera clickers, and "We gave them a sense of shame." The fact of the matter was that because, customarily, prostitutes were the only ones who covered their breasts, there was reluctance to do so when President Sukarno ordered the wearing of blouses in 1949. However, fashion played its part; the Western cinema had its influence in making brassieres modish; the president undoubtedly had charisma; and it also helped that Sukarno's mother was a Balinese. Sukarno's concern was with the West's associating bare bosoms with primitiveness and permissiveness, which were not what he wanted in the image abroad of the brand-new Republic of Indonesia.

It would be a mistake, though, to think that if the photographs I took of young women carrying offerings on their heads to a temple festival had been taken forty years ago they would have shown them "topless". On such formal occasions the Balinese have always liked to dress up in finery that swathes the torso.

A French cinematographer who went to Bali shortly after Sukarno issued his edict found the older women still showing their breasts—"So many empty bags!" he wrote, and, "In accordance with the new law, charming flowered blouses have made their appearance. Beauty is no loser in this exchange, far from it, and sex-obsessed travellers are less numerous in Bali."[3]

Which is one way of looking at what has been widely regarded as a deprivation.

AUSTRALIA, two thousand miles of the least-inhabited and least-habitable interior of the continent, moves under the plane wing like a diorama unrolling flatly thirty thousand feet below. It is 2.15 p.m. by the watch I'll shortly need to adjust, by putting it back three hours. We are dead centre, and I look for the

4

View from my room at the Bali Beach Inter-Continental hotel, Sanur, at high tide. Guests can go sailing with boatmen of the pictureque outriggers.

BALI

Author's Ektachromes

At the Segara Village Hotel, where I also stayed, some accommodation derived its two-storeyed form from the traditional Balinese rice barns.

Ploughs, steel-tipped but still wooden, are drawn through the mud of the ricefields by humped Brahman (zebu) cattle, or by water-buffaloes.

BALI   Author's Ektachromes

Harvesting the rice is done by men and women together walking through the crop and cutting it, not with sickles but with small hooked knives.

marvellous red monolith of Ayers Rock; but a rare canopy of overcast down there blots out all view of The Rock and Alice Springs. Less than two hours later we leave Australia at Derby on its nor'-west shoulder.

The Dutchman in the next seat is sleeping off the gin-tonic that preceded luncheon's *hors d'oeuvres*, and the German riesling with the chicken roasted Indonesian style with grated coconut and grilled peanuts, and more champagne with his ice-cream cake while I was having the good French burgundy with the Dutch cheese. I am rescued from sleepyheadedness by the arrival of afternoon tea; and although one associates Indonesia, or at least Java, with coffee, this tea tastes particularly good.

A vast and shipless sea is being drunk up as vapour by a blazing tropical sun and looks less like water than a mass of blue air. An hour and twenty minutes flying over it from Australia's edge will bring up landfall Bali. One island of Indonesia's three thousand inhabited islands, Bali is slotted between Java and Lombok in a chain or band of islands so long that if the archipelago were up in the North Atlantic it would stretch right across that ocean from Quebec in Canada to Cork in Ireland.

Although Indonesia is thought of as being part of South-east Asia, much of it lies closer to Australia than it does to continental Asia. Bali is closer to Perth than the Western Australian capital is to Sydney—which was one reason why a Perth accountant I was to meet had taken his family to Indonesia on holiday instead of across to Sydney or Surfers Paradise. They had flown from Perth to Djakarta direct and were seeing something of Java as well as Bali, which is more than most Bali-goers do.

It seemed a pity, for Australians in particular, to see no more of Indonesia than the island that, although it is undoubtedly the best place for the tourist to go, is not at all typical of the neighbour nation that contains 120 million people, 77 million of them on Java. In terms of population Indonesia is the fifth largest country in the world. There are more Indonesians than Japanese.

At two thirty (Bali time) the clouds that lolled on the northern horizon showed that they had land underneath them. The highest peak of this land poked up through a cloud, its cone like a dark island on a white sea. This was Gunung Agung, the

5

godhead mountain the Balinese look to worshipfully. It rises 10,000 feet.

For five hundred years or more (the records are imprecise) Agung was supposed to be a dead volcano. In 1963 it roared into eruption and took the lives of about 1,600 villagers living on its sides. The gods up there must be angry with them, the people of the region said and, blaming themselves and others for the disaster, they made many offerings and sacrifices.

The gods of which the great mountain is believed to be the home are the Hindu deities, Brahma, Vishnu (locally, Wisnu) and Shiva (or Siwa); and ancestors who have become as gods also live on Agung's summit or in the heaven over it. To the Balinese the higher a place is the holier it is. So they don't think much of the sea: it has not only such menaces as sharks and sea-snakes but its depths, they believe, are full of demons. I saw only one Balinese swimming in the sea, although they are a cleanly people much given to bathing in streams. Not much fish is eaten, fishermen's boats are relatively few, and so are any boats except the decorative praus that take tourists out on joy-rides from the beaches at Sanur, where the big hotel is, four miles from Denpasar and ten from the airport.

From the air the hotel was no more than a great white box, the island scene did not look particularly luxuriant, and as we came in to land the airport looked rather messy. Second impressions were better.

From a first-class room's balcony on the sixth floor of the Hotel Bali Beach the view was picture-postcard resort tropicality with coconut palms galore and the low tide baring a coral reef out where the deeper blue began. Next morning the scene was better still. The tide had filled in the shallow reaches with sea that was bluer than the bright sky. The sun had turned the beach sand to tawny gold and decorated the grounds with the palm fronds' shadow patterns. Outrigger praus with long white sails like tipped-up triangles were skimming about the sea that was still only hip-deep to a lone fisherman in a mushroom hat who was casting a seine net.

The Hotel Bali Beach crowd was very cosmopolitan, not just the Orient's usual Americans with a sprinkling of Europeans, Australians and Japanese. The French, though a long way from

6

France, were there in force, and so were the West Germans, and more than a few Latin-Americans.

When the hotel—which was built as part of Japanese war reparations—opened in 1966 it was so poorly patronized that at one early stage there were nearly a thousand staff looking after seventeen guests. Five years later it was so heavily booked that when I was there the management said that, owing to people vacating rooms late in the day and others moving in, the room occupancy rate was an extraordinary 103 per cent—beyond a hotelier's wildest dreams.

Big international-style hotels are often criticized as being too ostentatiously conventionalized and too expensive. Yet enough people want, and are prepared to pay for, all the amenities and services such places offer. The only question with much point to it, then, is: Which ones are particularly good *of their kind*? Five of the hotels I was enabled to stay at on this trip were either of, or affiliated with, the Inter-Continental chain, which was first recommended to me in 1967 by an airline executive who travels a lot. I have found them first rate. I spent six nights at the Hotel Bali Beach and then went to a Balinese hotel that wasn't luxurious, but it was very pleasant and much lower in its price. (In 1972 the minimum daily tariff for a double room at the Bali Beach was $24 plus 21 per cent, service charge and tax.)

I was in Bali in late August and early September. The best months extend from May to November. There is less rain in this season: I had only one wet day. I expected Bali to be hotter and much more humid than it was. The heat is tempered by the south-east tradewind, which blows up from the direction of Australia and is spoken of as the "Australian wind".

The muddy-legged musician

MUNTAG is a man of Bali, a ricefarmer. He has a wife (only rich men can afford more than one) and three children. His house is in one of the *kampong* compounds we pass on sightseeing tours of the island. We don't see the houses unless we go through the wall that runs beside the road. A mud wall about six feet high is topped with a ridge of rough thatch. It is broken at intervals with gateless entrances.

The walled roads of Bali, like peaceful lanes extended, are restful to our eyes that have been busied with the clutter and thrust of urban scenes. The pale-brown mud is like a harmonious outgrowth of the earth and hardly less natural than the green abundance over and about the wall—the coconut-palms and bigger trees like the breadfruit, the velvety-petalled frangipani, papayas shading their fruits with leaves like splayed green hands, banana-palms and, not least, the plumy grace of the bamboo.

Although Muntag could not imagine life without bamboo— it makes the walls of his house, the frame of his bed, the bell-like basket that houses his fighting cock, and flutes and hats and irrigation pipelines—he would never plant bamboo near his house. It is one of the taboos that Muntag lives by, one of the unlucky things to do, like going to sleep with your feet facing north.

Muntag's house (or his father's, for his parents share it) is not one *balé* (pavilion) but several. The main sleeping room, which is windowless and dark, is separate from two others, and the kitchen is separate again and so is the granary. As well, there is an enclosure with the family altars for offerings to the ancestors. These and the main balé are on the side of the compound nearest the sacred mountain, Gunung Agung. All the roofs of house pavilions are thatch of *lalang* grass tied to bamboo framework. The thatches of the shrines and altars, sometimes one roof, sometimes roof upon roof in the style of the pagoda and called a *meru*, are of sugar-palm fibre that turns black; and these, being higher than the wall, are what you notice from the road.

A neighbour of Muntag's who has ten acres of riceland (Muntag has only two) has his house on much the same plan, but with front porches to each balé; and instead of just altars he has a family temple of rosy red brick, ornate with carvings in grey siltstone of demonic-looking guardians.

All the compounded houses together form a *desa*, a village, and this is run by a council, consisting of all the married men,

8

called the *bandjar*. Indonesia's form of national government may be dictated by the Army, but Bali has long had this village-level democracy. The bandjar has its own large balé, which is not only a meeting-place but serves as concert hall and theatre when performances aren't out in the open, as they usually are.

AT DAYLIGHT the village wakes up to the gamecocks' crowing. Muntag puts his wicker-caged rooster out where it can see the village activity before he goes off to the *sawah*, the ricefield, usually without eating anything and taking his breakfast of boiled rice with him. He will come home in the hot middle of the day, and eat a bigger meal, again of rice, salted and spiced or chili-peppered. He doesn't use a knife, fork or spoon and a section of banana leaf serves as a plate that, when discarded, may be eaten by a sway-backed black pig, or a dog. The scavenging dogs, all mange and scars and rib cage, eat anything, even ordure. Nobody feeds them or is kind to them. To ill-treat them, though, is risky because they may be the reincarnation of someone who is malignant. The dogs eat up offerings set out to placate evil spirits. It is believed necessary to make such offerings, as well as to supplicate good spirits.

The growing season for rice is in Bali continuous and the rich volcanic soil yields two crops a year. Muntag may be planting out rice in the morning on one irrigation-flooded terrace, and in the afternoon harvesting across the dry earth of another terrace or field.

Muntag's wife, Klemit, takes part in the harvesting, and also in the planting nowadays: it used to be that only the men could do that. Rice is the very staff of life and there are reverential, ritualized procedures about how the first plants should be set out in a certain pattern. There are little altars in the fields for offerings to Sri, wife of Wisnu and goddess of agriculture and fertility.

To prepare his field for planting, Muntag yokes a fawn-coloured cow or bull (in northern Bali more use is made of the water buffalo) to a wooden, steel-shared plough. It is an arduous job, rice cultivation, the workbeast sinking down to its hocks and Muntag calf-deep in the mud.

When he comes home in the late afternoon he washes his

9

mud-caked legs and bathes his body in the stream that runs past the village. Naked he bathes, but modestly cups his genitals with a hand. He puts on a clean sarong and, perhaps, a shirt. He takes his fighting cock from its wicker cage and, cradling it in his arms like a baby and talking to it, he goes to where some of the other men are already squatted on their haunches by the roadside, fondling their birds, massaging their legs and stroking their long plumes. The petted gamecocks welcome this daily interlude in the solitary and celibate constraint that feeds aggressiveness with frustration. Their owners are concerned to encourage the viciousness in their natures, so that they will be the readier to attack when their time comes to fight. Nature's fighting equipment—the left-leg spur—is cut off and is replaced with a thin lancet-sharp steel blade about five inches long. With this a cock's first strike may stab the other one deep and fatally, or it may carve it open. I detest cockfighting.

To Muntag cockfighting is sport and gambling. He bets on it just as, in our society, all kinds of men bet on horse races. I've known musicians who were avid punters. However, they made music more often than they made bets because musicianship was their livelihood. It isn't Muntag's but, more often than he is at a cockfight, this ricefarmer is to be found making music with the village orchestra, the *gamelan*.

As to education, Muntag did not finish primary school. He cannot read a note of music, nor can any of the other ricefarmers in this orchestra of twenty-five men. It is the gamelan of the bandjar and some of its instruments were in the village, handed down: others the bandjar has had to buy. They are, by Balinese standards, very costly, such instruments as the ten-gong *trompong* or the *reyong* of thirteen bronze gongs like upside-down bowls with knobby bottoms that are beaten with padded sticks. The metallophones are struck with little hammers and have sounding tubes of bamboo under the xylophone-style metal plates. Then there are the long drums and the cymbals that sound like their name, *tjeng-tjeng*. There are also flutes and a kind of violin.

Gamelan music does not "wail" as some Eastern music does in Western ears. It is vigorous, melodious and, at its best, exciting.

10

This GAMELAN has played for the dance drama—which Muntag's village does so well—at the Hotel Bali Beach. The first time Muntag went there it was with several other men from the village to see the positioning on the outdoor stage and set up the larger instruments. It was in the late afternoon and, near the stage, guests were still disporting themselves in the swimming-pool or were stretched out beside it, sunning. Muntag was shocked. Men and women were not only swimming together and lying together, but these white women—with no more shame than a Balinese woman felt about uncovering her breasts in a man's presence—revealed their thighs.

The audience the gamelan played for at the hotel dines in the open air in front of the stage and again Muntag was surprised at the difference in *adat* (custom, traditional behaviour). The men and women dined together, which would never happen in the kampong. A distinct odour came from where the tourists were dining: to Muntag it was an odd smell and he wouldn't have called it pleasant. But the most peculiar thing was that, when the performance finished, just about everybody in the audience smacked their hands together, making a noise so loud it was rather frightening. Applause is not customary in the village, any more than paying to see a performance is.

The diners paid an extra charge to see the dance-drama performance with gamelan music (and when I was there it was so popular that you needed to reserve a table). What the hotel paid the performers is known at least in relation to the *legong* dancers and the orchestra from the village of Sesetan, because an American anthropologist, Philip McKean, made a special study in 1971 of the effects of tourism on Balinese culture.[4] There was a flat fee of 6,000 rupiahs (about $A150 at that time). The profit was used by the Sesetan *bandjar* to buy extra riceland or to improve the meeting hall or the temples. McKean reported that such material improvement "did not lead to crass commercialism or secularism". The traditional society was not weakened by it, he said. This anthropologist found no support for what he called "the presumed expectation that Bali will soon be 'ruined' ".

"In fact," McKean wrote, "it may be possible for an audience of tourists to act as a patron of the arts", and he asked, "Is it

11

entirely unlikely that tourists, some of them discriminating, will encourage a flowering of dance, music, painting, carving and ritual performance?" In Sesetan village, ". . . the excellence of the local gamelan, intended for tourists, is now proudly displayed at local celebrations. Instead of diminishing indigenous culture, the presence and promise of tourists seems to have enhanced it."

A more notable anthropologist had said earlier of the Balinese adaptation to tourism: "It is the opposite case from that which we are apt to expect to deplore, when, with the advent of foreign tourists whose pocketbooks are heavy, the ceremonial dances and rites of a people are secularized, cheapened and robbed of their meaning to become a 'tourist show'. Such an instance of adaptation revealed a strength in the Balinese scheme of things which accounted in great part for its survival under changing influences . . . the adaptation was painless, even re-vivifying to the existing system, for it brought fresh interest and excitement to their life . . . ."[5]

Jacques Chegaray, the French film-maker, wrote in his book published in 1953:[3] "Balinese art, which was dormant, has had a brilliant revival with the recent influx of tourists, mainly Americans . . . . It is fashionable to criticize the hurried tourists who, between planes, visit the whole island in three days; yet it is because of them and their constantly growing demand that thousands of Balinese woodcarvers make a living. What previously could only be the occupation of the labourers' leisured hours, has now become a rewarding profession. Some idealists deplore this state of affairs. I feel that one ought rather to rejoice at it."

Critics of tourism argue that environments such as Bali must be conserved, unchanged, without considering whether the people might welcome change that alleviates poverty such as is commonly the lot of exotic communities. It is for the "cultured peasants" of Bali to say—not for us to say—whether they want to remain in a state of cultural peasantry.

"Native customs should never be interfered with", is the advocacy of bright-eyed amateur anthropologists who hold that the less native peoples' lives are impinged upon by our civilization the happier they always are. Are these romantics really prepared to chide the colonial Dutch for getting rid of such a custom as the Balinese form of Hindu suttee? The widows of a dead *radja* or prince were expected to sacrifice themselves by leaping into his funeral pyre. The practice persisted into this century: the last such immolations happened in 1903.

KLEMIT, the wife of Muntag, had some training when she was a girl of six as a *legong* dancer. Legongs are always young. They have to retire when they reach puberty.

Klemit did not show herself to be specially talented. Moreover, her fingers were rather too short and her eyes not quite big and expressive enough. Had her skill and endowments made her first-class she would have certainly made a better match than Muntag. They were married when she was eighteen and he was twenty-three.

Their marriage was, as many Balinese marriages are, preceded by an "elopement". The couple usually run off—for this part it is fashionable to hire a taxi—to the house of a friend of the groom where they stay for a day or two while the bride's parents go through the motions of concern but are usually quite in favour of the match. The marriage will have been consummated before they return to the bride's parents, who are by then arranging the wedding feast and have sent for the *pedanda*, the priest.

Before Muntag and Klemit married their teeth had to be filed level. This is regarded as not only aesthetically (and also morally) improving but as good insurance against not being reincarnated as a dog or some other long-toothed animal. There is a similar fear with babies. They are never allowed to crawl. If a baby goes on all fours like an animal, in the next life that is what it may become. So until it can walk, the child must be carried. Little girls do much baby-lugging.

Children in Bali are indulged: in our society there is much more scolding and hectoring of infants. Slapping a child is almost unknown: that could injure its tender spirit. Because the spirit is believed to be centred in the cranium, the tourist visitor, who is understandably enchanted with Balinese children, should refrain from patting any on the head. Parents regard this practice as dangerous, and the children don't like it, though they are not

13

so impolite as to cry, *"Djangan!"* ("Don't!")

Formerly, a great misfortune in the ordinary Balinese family was for the mother to give birth to boy-and-girl twins. Twins of the same sex were all right (although men generally desired sons and were unlikely to welcome the arrival of a duo of daughters). The belief was that twins of different sexes had been incestuous within the womb. This was pollution for the village and calamity for the parents, who had to pay the considerable cost of purification and have their house where the birth took place pulled down or burnt, and live for a stated time outside the village, usually in the cemetery, as pariahs. This particularly stupid and distress-causing superstition no longer has much prevalence. If dissimilar twins were born to a noble family, the parents' being high caste made it all right: indeed, such a birth was a good omen and welcomed. High-caste twins would *never* commit pre-natal incest!

Caste does not mean what it used to in Bali, but it still means a good deal, even though the tourist visitor may not be conscious that a caste system exists. There are four castes. The low caste is Sudra and to this the great majority of Balinese (ninety per cent according to Blackwood[6]) belong. The other three castes are more or less aristocratic. In ascending order, they are the Wesias, who are the merchant caste, and usually the Wesia men have the title prefix *Gusti* to their names; then the Satryas, the princely and military caste whose prefix titles include *Anak Agung, Tjorkorde* and *Ratu*; and the highest caste is that of the Brahmanas (equivalent of Brahmins in India) who were the high priests and the judges, and were supposed to be above commercial gain, but nowadays Brahmanas are to be found prospering in business: their names are prefixed with *Ida Bagus* in the case of men, *Ida Ayu* for women. It is still forbidden for a man to marry a woman of higher caste.

Balinese Hinduism is fairly accommodating as to food. A priest and his family (priests marry) can eat duck or goat, but not pork or beef. The ordinary Balinese can eat any of those meats, when he can afford them. The great delicacy for wedding feasts and the like is turtle meat. But most people are very happy with roast suckling pig, *babi guling*.

The fighting cock killed in the arena goes into the pot.

14

Fighting crickets are kept as well as fighting cocks, and the losing crickets are fried, as are dragonflies the children catch with glue on a stick.

Sacrifices have to be made when the gods show disfavour and need placating. Geese, chickens, pigeons then have their necks cut—and some dogs. Sacrificed poultry is eaten, but dog meat is not, except in the villages of some inlanders who are looked down upon as hillbillies.

However, Balinese Hinduism is not given to blood sacrifices to anything like the extent one encounters in the Hindu kingdom of Nepal, where a new motor lorry won't be driven until, as an accident-preventive rite, the bonnet has been smeared with the blood of a goat. Another difference is that Balinese temples are relatively empty of idols. The figures carved on gateways are not gods but guardians against evil spirits. The temple is not primarily a residing place of gods in effigy, but a place where the gods *visit* to receive offerings and to hear supplications—which are made through the priests, not as prayers to worshipped images. "There are more temples in relation to the population than anywhere else on earth," says Blackwood,[6] but adds, "there are no temples in the normal sense." The Balinese don't go to their temples as Christians go to churches, but only on festival occasions. But they go constantly to their shrines.

The women are for ever making offerings. Every house shrine must have its daily offering, which may be only a pretty arrangement of a few grains of rice and a flower or two on a tiny platter of palm-leaf. For an important festival, an offering may consist of fruits piled four feet high to look beautifully decorative. Fixed in position on a base, the arrangement is carried on the head, resting on a pad of a towel folded ringwise. Klemit, who has been carrying things on her head since she was three years old, performs this balancing feat with poised assurance and a beautifully straight back.

When an offering is presented to the priest at the temple it may be accompanied with what is called a *lamak*. This is a hanging not unlike an unrolled scroll. It is made entirely of palm leaves of different colours. The simpler form is a cut-out showing light green leaf under dark green; but an elaborate one

15

may be in dyed-leaf colours, and the intricate patterns that are cut in the leaf or pinned on it with slivers of bamboo are so decorative that *lamak* must be ranked as a Balinese artform.

Painting is the prerogative of the male. So is sculpture. Girls, as legongs, may become the most admired of all dancers—but females are not allowed to make music.

Male repugnance at woman's "uncleanness" at her menstrual time means in Bali that for about a week she is not only forbidden to go inside a temple but she cannot enter her own kitchen or the granary of the house.

Pigs are always fed and tended by the women, and so are chickens. Any money a woman makes by selling her pigs and chickens at the market is accounted as hers and does not have to be rendered to her husband.

Ducks are looked after by young boys or old men, and they are taken out each morning to forage in the wet *sawahs* for small rice eels and other food. They never stray far from a bamboo staff with a flutter of rag at the top, which the duckherd carries and plants in the ground. In the evening the ducks gather at the staff for their waddling march in formation back to the village.

The ducks being brought in at evening, the boy behind them with the bamboo staff not hurrying their slow-rolling gait as they move along a narrow bank between two ricefields, like a foreground frieze to the evening sky glow—this is truly a picture that says Bali, and one that, alas, I did not manage to get, satisfactorily, inside my camera.

Dances, and trances

OF THE ARTS of Bali the most distinctive is the dance. Tourists have become aware of this and for them many dances are performed, sometimes at the hotels, mainly in the villages.

What follows is about some of the dances, or dance dramas, visitors are likely to see.

16

RAMAYANA

The story of Prince (later King) Rama is an epic poem of India that is almost as ancient as the *Odyssey* of Greece. Parts of the *Ramayana* would appear to have been danced as ballet for more than a thousand years before Marco Polo set European foot in these islands at the end of the thirteenth century; and today's tourists see dancers enact the same story on the stage at the Bali Beach hotel.

If a Balinese waiter, in the course of bringing food to the out-door diners, sees a princely hunter run across the stage after a dancer representing a golden deer, he knows that the deer will be shot and, in dying, turn into a kinsman of the Demon King. If he sees the prince involved with a monkey he knows that the king of the monkeys is about to become Rama's potent friend and will aid the rescue of his beloved, Sita, with monkey armies under the command of the monkey general, Hanuman. The waiter will have seen it or heard it so often before.

Balinese children know every *Ramayana* character. As they grow up and learn to appreciate the finer points of interpretation, they are—like Western balletomanes seeing their seventeenth *Swan Lake*—no longer concerned with how the story unfolds but with how well each role is danced and characterized.

Under these critical circumstances the performers have to be good, and the ones I saw at the hotel *were* good. Aesthetically, I should think, most Westerners would expect the typical Balinese ballerina to be slimmer, less rounded and "well covered", more like the sylphs we are used to seeing on the ballet stage. Doubtless Balinese reaction to the ethereal Pavlova, whose chest was almost skeletal and whose arms were like bones become white rubber, would have been that the poor woman must have been starved of her rice ration.

The principal *Ramayana* dancers were glitteringly costumed in rich brocades.

LEGONG

What Covarrubias regarded as the best of all Balinese dances and "the archetype of the delicate and feminine" is performed by children. Usually there are three girls, and they may all be aged under twelve. At puberty they cease to be *legongs*.

The little legongs are so made up with powdered cheeks and drawn-on eyebrows, and such ornately patterned brocades swathe their small bodies so sophisticatedly, they look less like children than like miniaturized women. Also it seems not quite believable that juvenile girls could do what these do—their bodies arched above out-thrust little bottoms; their fingers curving back and quivering, or flicking a fan so fast that the movement blurs like birds' wings beating; their so-slender necks suddenly and disconcertingly acting like double-jointed fingers and jerking their heads from side to side, from shoulder to shoulder almost, at the same time as they make side-snapping movements with their eyes.

The dance's story is, to the Western visitor, of little account in legong: the manner is what matters. It is usually a story from the *Malat*, the Balinese equivalent of the *Arabian Nights*, about the lustful King of Lasem and the Princess Lankesari, his beautiful prisoner whom he seeks to seduce. The third dancer—the two legongs' "attendant" called the *tjondong*—wears wings of gilded leather and plays the bird of ill omen that brings disaster to the king.

I saw a very good legong performance at Tandjung Sari (the name means "cape of flowers"), a highly-rated Sanur resort hotel with beach-side bungalows in traditional Balinese style, accommodation that some people prefer to the international-style luxury of the Hotel Bali Beach. Tandjung Sari gets excellent dancers for its evening performances, which are held indoors, and it had engaged what was reputedly Bali's best *gamelan* from the village of Peliatan.

BARIS

This is the warrior dance (the word *baris* means a military file or formation). Solo *baris* is particularly vigorous, in a highly stylized way. Any Westerner who, watching baris, thinks he could do it, quite possibly could if, as a test of his muscles' flexibility, he can do this: with knees spread wide apart and in line with the body, sit on his heels.

As well as having such physical prowess, a baris dancer needs to be an actor capable of registering a whole range of emotions,

18

including fierceness such as Covarrubias describes: "As the music grows more violent the dancer becomes more and more tense, raising himself on his toes until he gives the impression of growing in height; his eyes seem ready to jump from their sockets, his whole body trembles, making the flowers in his headdress shake violently. So raised on his toes and with his whole body at high nervous tension, he slaps his thigh and points an accusing finger at his enemy as with wild yells of 'Wah! Adoh! Adoh!' he draws his kris. . . ."[2] A baris dance commonly ends in a duel.

Sometimes the Balinese idea of what the well-dressed warrior should wear is delightfully unmilitary. One baris group had not only high pointed headdresses decked with silver flowers, but they wore stoles of what looked like pink chiffon.

TOPENG

This is dance-mime done with masks. The most skilful *topeng* actors are often old men who are still, mentally and physically, so skilled as actors that when they put on a mask, be it the face of a king or a clown, they are completely that character.

Like the *Noh* dance masks of Japan, the best *topeng* masks of Bali are works of art that collectors treasure. The visitor can see some good ones in the Denpasar Museum.

BARONG

Although this is billed as a dance, usually as "Barong and Kris Dance", the dance part is incidental. The performance is primarily a drama: one might almost say melodrama, but the accent here is not so much on the sensational as on the supernatural. Religion and entertainment overlap. The mythical animal *Barong* is no mere theatrical creation like a pantomime horse. Grotesque though he is, the Barong embodies the principle of Good, and he is protective. A Balinese community that doesn't have a Barong is likely to feel spiritually poor and insecure.

Evil, it is believed, can be wrought magically by the monstrous witch-queen *Rangda*. In the drama Rangda fights with the

19

Barong. People who believe that *leyaks,* witches, exist—and I was assured by a well-educated Balinese that most people did, and he did himself—also believed that a malefic influence could emanate from the stage Rangda with the awful fanged mask. So it was considered unwise to show Rangda being actually vanquished by the Barong, and thought just as well to propitiate her with offerings or a sacrifice. The performance is likely to end with the blood of a chicken being sprinkled on the ground; but at the Barong I saw we were spared this.

The village of Batubulan had a good outdoor setting, against a rosy-brick temple façade with stone carvings. The Hotel Bali Beach collected $2 for admission and $1.50 for two-way transportation. The show lasted an hour, from nine to ten o'clock in the morning. A good *gamelan* played for it. Some other villages also put on Barong performances for tourists and no two versions are quite the same, so what you see does not necessarily correspond to the programme story you are given (written in English by a Balinese who was having grammar and spelling trouble). The story was, in any case, rather bewilderingly full of bewitchments and people assuming the forms of animals. But there was plenty of action, and the movements of a man in a monkey suit and mask could not have been more monkey-like. The monkey is the Barong's friend.

The Barong is long, sway-backed and hairy and its face suggests a lion whose mother was frightened by a Chinese dragon. Two men fill the Barong costume. The great mask head has a movable jaw that opens and clacks, and the Barong's forepart is made more strikingly gaudy by being inset with many small mirrors.

The terrible Rangda is the ultimate in female grotesquerie. She has very ugly long dugs, prognathous jaws full of outsize teeth flanked with enormous fangs, and her tongue hangs red in semblance of consuming fire.

The Barong-*v*-Rangda fight is a no-decision bout that ends what the programme calls Act Six. Then the Barong brings on his henchmen to attack Rangda. These six men are bare to the waist and each has a kris (long two-edged dagger with a wavy blade).

Rangda's power is such that she is able to make the attackers

20

In a trance dance (sanghyang) the man squatting on his play-horse made of palmleaf, in front of a priest, "cantered" barefoot through a fire, unharmed.

BALI   Author's Ektachromes

Ramayana—the story of the Hindu legendary hero, Prince Rama—is danced on an outdoor stage in the grounds of the Bali Beach Inter-Continental hotel.

Baris (the warrior) dance in two forms, ABOVE *and* BELOW. *Movements are brilliantly stylized, and the costumes most decorative.*
Author's Ektachromes

BALI
Legong, the dance that calls for so much artistry, is performed by quite young girls, who dance it only until they reach puberty.

turn their krisses against themselves. But, as each man tries to stab his kris into his chest, the Barong counters black magic with white and so hardens the men's flesh that the kris cannot penetrate. There is the dramatic final spectacle of the kris dancers ostensibly straining every muscle, their faces contorted as they strive to force the sharp points into their chests.

"In most plays" (says the *Guide to Bali*[7]), "this phenomenal self-stabbing is enacted while the kris dancers are in trance."

At this performance I did not get the impression that the kris dancers were in a state of trance. What they did—and it was first-rate as theatre—seemed to me to come within the scope of very good play acting.

My impression that trance was not involved could have been wrong. But trance is a subject best considered after the next dances.

SANGHYANG

This is spoken of as the trance dance. *Sanghyang* is a religious term meaning "spirit" and the dance's whole import used to be religious. Sometimes it served as an exorcism ritual when there were epidemics.

There are at least ten kinds of sanghyang. One Saturday night I saw two kinds, with other tourists brought by bus to the village of Belega. The setting was a bare space in front of a temple gateway, without much light. There was no *gamelan*, but two choruses were seated on the ground. One was of girls in dark red sarongs and patterned blue tops that left their shoulders bare. The other chorus was of men, bare to the waist and their loins wrapped in the black-and-white check cloth that is a sacred pattern and often seen draping guardian figures at shrines. Each man wore a scarlet hibiscus behind his right ear.

The first dance is the *dedari* (heavenly nymphs) *sanghyang*. The girls' chorus sings an invocation that two beautiful nymphs will descend from heaven and enter into two young girls. These two, who look to be about eleven years old have been dressed up as *legong* dancers. They have been brought from the temple where offerings have been made by a priest who has placed before each girl a brazier of incense. The smoke rises about them and the girls are suffused with the incense and, we are told, are now in a state of trance.

These children dance. They go through movements of the legong, not dancing it well. Their eyes are closed. Their movements are somnambulistic rather than precise. But how can they dance legong at all when, we are assured, they have never had a single lesson in this dance it takes girls years to learn? The Balinese answer is that they can dance the legong because the spirits of the heavenly nymphs have come down and entered into them and taken control of their bodies.

The two girls are lifted onto the shoulders of two men and, balancing there, are carried. While they are being carried they do dance movements with their arms and they even lean their bodies backwards. On the ground they dance again in legong style.

Then, first one and then the other, these girls fall down. They just crumple and keel over in the dirt. The priest appears and sprinkles them with holy water. The girls, who have appeared to be unconscious, revive. They stand up, and women who are probably their mothers lead them away.

"I CONFESS to having been much affected the first time I witnessed the performance," Jacques Chegaray wrote of the *sanghyang dedari*. "Unfortunately, a month later I saw the ceremony again, and it was then that I realized that the whole affair was a perfect piece of play acting, of the same order as the kris dance. I could not help noticing that the little girls executed precisely the same steps and movements as in a well-learned lesson. And when at the end they woke up, the same little girl lingered in half sleep the necessary five minutes and woke with the same gestures. I felt it was a well-rehearsed mime."[3]

Legong, says Chegaray, is daily fare to any little Balinese girl and, as for the balancing on a man's shoulders, that was a trick easily taught.

Before bringing in the most authoritative researcher of trance in Bali, let us look at the second "trance dance" I saw. This was called the *djaran* (horse) *sanghyang*.

A man clad in white except for the black-and-white-check "sacred" cloth round his hips, kneels in front of a seated priest who has a brazier of incense. The smoke from this rises about

22

the man, who inhales it, and he begins to sway gently back and forth.

Now the man gets astride a "horse"—a play-horse fashioned of palmleaf, its decorative form curving back between the rider's legs and rising to a high, plumy tail. The chorus of the seated men (who are called the *ketjak*) begins. As though obedient to this chanted sound, the man rides off on the play-horse at a cantering gait. He rides towards a fire that has been kindled earlier out of dried husks of coconuts. The fire blazed high and it is now a heap of glowing coals.

The man rides his palm-horse right into this fire and through it, scattering the red-hot material with his bare feet. He does this several times, without faltering, and apparently without burning his feet.

The chanting of the male chorus ceases. The horseman stops prancing round. He moves unsteadily. Then he falls to the ground: he appears to have fainted. The priest sprinkles holy water on him, three times. And, in the words of the roneoed program, "he gets his senses again". He has danced as he did and gone through the fire unharmed, in a state of trance: or so we are told.

TRANCE

TRANCE is an integral part of Balinese religion. Attached to the temples are holy men or women called *sadegs* who are adept at going into trance. When they are in a state of trance, it is believed, the gods enter them. The sadegs are the mediums who "bring the gods down".

Unless the gods are brought down people cannot make their offerings and supplications to them, through the priests. Some of the priests, also, can go into trance. On trance, then, much communication with the gods depends.

I may, in fact do, deny that these gods exist. My disbelief has no bearing whatever on what belief may give rise to in others. These *sadegs* identify with their gods, and they even speak for them. Similarly, a hypnotist's subject may show all the signs of intoxication after drinking a glass of what he has been told by the hypnotist is whisky. The fact that you and I know the glass contained only water is irrelevant.

Anyone who has seen a person in a state of hypnotic trance—perhaps in a cataleptic condition with the body stretched rigid between two chairs—will need no convincing that there *is* such a thing as a state of trance, and that it can result in quite dramatic changes in behaviour, mentally and physically.

That is not to say that the French cinematographer Chegaray could not have been right in saying that trance was not involved in the little girls' *sanghyang dedari* dancing or the kris dancers' self-stabbing routine in the *Barong* performance. As I said, I saw no necessity for the kris dancers to be in trance to perform as they did; and whether or not trance was involved in that particular performance I still don't know. My guess would be that it was not. But I must now believe that trance is frequently involved in the *Barong* and is always, or nearly always, involved in the *sanghyang* dances.

My scepticism did not survive reading a book I wished I had read before I went to Bali. *Trance in Bali*, by Jane Belo,[5] is patently the work of a good anthropologist; and those front-rankers in the field, Margaret Mead and Gregory Bateson, participated in this study.

In one form of *sanghyang* investigated, a man who went in trance identified with a pig. He walked on all fours, scratched himself against buildings, drank slobberingly from a trough, grunted and squealed and wallowed in mud. He also became ill subsequently because in his pig state he ate a quantity of excreta. (A case is on record, but not in Belo's book, of a pig trancer trying to copulate with a sow.) Other *sanghyang* trancers acted as though they were a monkey, a puppy, a snake. Playing such roles they described as being "delightful". The investigators found that animal-like behaviour, low behaviour such as a Balinese would ordinarily avoid as degrading, "becomes in the state of trance pleasurable".

Jane Belo thought such trance behaviour could possibly explain why Balinese who normally appeared the most good-tempered of people, particularly equable and slow to anger, should suddenly run *amok*. If they are customarily repressed, ". . . it is not impossible that when the Balinese go in trance and have a violent fit of what they think of as anger, they are indulging in the luxury of an orgy of unfamiliar emotion."

The part trance played in the kris dance was investigated. It was not always easy to decide whether the dancers were acting or were genuinely in trance because in Bali "not only would the entranced behave as if he were acting but the actor would behave almost as if he were in trance". However, it was thought dangerous to pretend to be in a trance. As a *sadeg* put it, "If one is not in trance and falls down as if in trance, he can break his arm. Once unconscious [in trance] even though he falls nothing happens. . . . He picks up fire, his hands are not burnt."

Trancers, including kris dancers, were seen to take hot coals in their hands, even lick the coals or put them in the mouth, apparently without being burned. The coals were from the brazier of incense. Being "smoked" was the standard way of going in trance.

The ritual "self stabbing" with the kris is called *ngurek*. Since it is not invariably done in a state of trance, it can hardly be said that the trance state is the dancer's protection from the kris piercing his chest. Reference is made to the pectoral muscles being flexed hard against the point of the kris, and to krisses being pressed so hard that they bent. Frenzy beyond what an actor could simulate is described as the state of some of the *ngurek* performers the anthropologists observed. Exceptional muscular rigidity was attested in cases of men trying to disarm a "possessed" one. All the same, one could wish for more evidence of what occurs physiologically. Mentally, there appears to be an overwhelming desire to perform this kris act. One young man who was known as a lecher said his desire for the kris was stronger than desire for a woman.

The self-wounding of a kris dancer—it happened rarely but was by no means unknown—was attributed to the man being *sebel* (unclean). A man whose wife gave birth was *sebel* for three days.

PERFORMANCES of *sanghyang dedari* by girls below the age of puberty were studied by the anthropologists. They affirm that the young girls had no *legong* training and that they were truly in trance when they danced.

Jane Belo wrote: "Once brought into trance, the little girls were able to dance not only 'as if they had been trained', but they were able to perform other feats unknown to the professional dancers; they could climb upon the shoulders of men who then move about with the little girls balanced and dancing high in the air; and they could dance on hot coals without feeling the heat."[5]

Photographs show the girls "falling limp as they go into trance" and a girl dancing while standing on a man's shoulders, "an extraordinary feat". Their dancing is described by Belo as somnambulistic, and sometimes the dancers "bump smack into each other". The girls' dancing on hot coals was not a feature of the dances studied in the Kintamani region; but it was filmed at another place. The Kintamani girls put their hands in the flames of the brazier.

There is a report of *sanghyang djaran*, the "horse" dance, with two tranced horsemen. Before they kicked the fire to pieces and stamped it all out with their bare feet, the men lay down and rolled in the fire.

In another form of *sanghyang* a man had one arm "smoked". Then he ran about collecting pieces of heavy firewood, which had been looped round with string, lifting them with his little finger. He constantly made involuntary rotating movements with one hand, for thirteen minutes. Then the tranced man was caught and examined by the chief psychiatrist of Java at that time, Dr P.M. van Wulfften Palthe. "The right arm was completely rigid from the elbow down, the muscles all contracted and appearing enormous."[5]

The eminent doctor considered the trance manifestations those of normal Balinese, not pathological types; but he did not believe that all Balinese could go in trance—only those of high emotionality, lively imagination, and a somewhat infantile psychic structure. He regarded the trance phenomena as being of a kind identified with hysteria rather than with schizophrenia.

KETJAK

This is the most arresting dance drama Bali has to offer. *Ketjak* is the name of the male chorus in the *sanghyang* and this dance extends the role of that chorus to a *Ramayana*-story presentation in which the number of men is increased to about

26

150. They provide such striking accompaniment that what the chorus does is much more remarkable than what is done by the solo dancers who come in and portray such *Ramayana* characters as Prince Rama, the Demon King Rawana, the Garuda bird and Hanuman the monkey general.

The "Monkey Dance" is what *Ketjak* is usually billed as in tourist programmes. All it has to do with monkeys is that, near the end, half the chorus become Hanuman's jabbering monkey army and the other half represent the enemy demons.

All the movements of the chorusmen are made without their ever rising to their feet from the sitting position. There is no accompanying orchestra: all the sound is vocal, and it is the sound as much as the movement that gives *Ketjak* its dramatic impact.

It is important to see a first-class performance. I saw two *Ketjaks*, and the one by Segara beach was clearly a case of the locals getting on the *Ketjak* bandwagon, cashing in on the tourist trade. It is possible that from such beginnings a good performance will develop. There were already three that were first class, at the villages of Bedulu, Bona and Peliatan.

I saw the Bedulu group in a special performance for delegates to an Asian Press convention, for whom the Governor of Bali gave a dinner. This was held at the best and most attractive Balinese-style restaurant on the island, Puri Suling (meaning Palace of Flutes) at Bedulu, about thirty miles north from the Hotel Bali Beach, and operated by that hotel's former food and beverages manager, Robert Hargrove, an American.

The setting for this *Ketjak* was specially atmospheric—it was in front of the carved entrance to a shrine cut into the rock and called (because it held an image of the elephant-headed Hindu god Ganesh) the Elephant Cave.

THE HUNDRED AND FIFTY MEN are seated, circle within circle, round a central space where a branched candelabrum of *naga* (sacred serpent) design holds up five small oil lamps. There is no other light. The night is moonless but starry. No breeze stirs the fronds of the coconut palms that rise in this natural amphitheatre. The air is balmy and carries a faint smell of incense and coconut oil.

The men are naked to the waist, their loins wrapped in the black-and-white check, and each has a red hibiscus tucked behind his right ear and a floret of white frangipani behind the left. Their torsoes gleam a rich dark brown in the oil flames' light.

The start is a shout that cracks the air. The chorus becomes charged with more energy than could ever be expected to emanate from the bodies of seated, earthbound men. Torsoes are dancing, shoulders jumping, muscles rippling—and they chant. "*Tjak, tjak, tjak! Tjak, tjak, tjak, tjak!*"

Now arms are upflung. Then the torsoes go forward, the arms outstretched. Three hundred pointed hands become something else—a vibrant mass of fluttering fingers, every finger shaking, dancing.

Heads are bowed, arms rested on the crossed legs' knees, but the stillness is only momentary. The men are bolt upright again, shoulders jumping, muscles rippling, and the aural impact seems even greater the second time as they chant again their *Tjak, tjak, tjak! Tjak, tjak, tjak, tjak, tjak!* Sound without resonance, hard and sharp as flint, it hammers the ear with excitement.

In the circle at the centre of this density of bodies, the solo dancers perform, depart, and others enter. Their presence and performance doesn't seem to matter much—the chorus, the *Ketjak*, is the show. Two dancing girls look lost in a forest of upflung hands. The Demon King has no movements to compete with a hundred and fifty men suddenly flinging themselves backwards, heads resting on the bellies of the men behind—or sideways so that they are coiled like a human rope.

And all the time there is this dramatic vocalization, ranging from hissing through to cries, and stabbing the night with the sound that seems to be articulated less by the mouths than the muscles of the men who do the staccato *Tjak, tjak, tjak!*

BALI   Author's Ektachromes

Ketjak Dance, ABOVE, *is danced seated and without music; but the vibrant arm and hand movements and staccato chant of "Tjak, tjak, tjak!" make it an outstanding performance.*

It is also called Monkey Dance. LEFT: *Hanuman, a warrior monkey, is about to leap from a tree into the circle,* BELOW.

BALI

The Barong, RIGHT, although grotesque, is believed in as the protector against the terrible witch, Rangda.

ABOVE: *The amazing Kris Dance. Rangda magically makes the Barong's men turn their daggers against themselves—but the Barong's magic hardens their flesh.*

OPPOSITE PAGE: *The temple's "split" gateway at Batubulan village makes a fine setting for the Barong dance drama.*

Author's Ektachromes

Gunung Agung, Bali's highest mountain and holy volcano—which in 1963 erupted, killing 1,600 villagers—rears its great head above a cloudbank.

BALI Author's Ektachromes

Gunung (Mount) Batur, also volcanic, was rumbling loudly and sending up, at five-minute intervals, a column of smoke from a small crater in its side.

Seeing more than Sanur

TOURISTS often prefer to be referred to as "travellers". Yet "tourist" is a perfectly respectable term, harking back to the Grand Tour of Europe, which only the rich could afford, before the last Napoleonic war. It simply means "one who tours". But many so-called tourists don't tour.

They just fly to an international-class luxury hotel, in Majorca one year, the Bahamas the next, Bali the year after, and spend nearly all their days sun-tanning, drink-sipping and socializing beside similar swimming-pools waved over by the same kind of palms. These people we probably should call "travellers", since all they do is travel to a place and, once there, do nothing to earn the name of "tourist". Well, it's their holiday. . . .

Of course, it is in the interests of such hotels to make the place so attractively comfortable that people are happy to stay within the purlieus and spend their money there. However, if guests want to tour, these big hotels make it easy for them to do so. Usually the hotel has its own tour booking service, and it also rents off-lobby offices to other tour operators, who are unlikely to get location within the hotel premises unless they are good.

At the Hotal Bali Beach there was Golden Bali Tours. I got to know and like its general manager, S. T. Lie, who seemed to me particularly alert and concerned to run a good service; and that was the impression the staff gave, too.

One of the tours I took with a GBT car and guide was to Besakih, the mother temple of Bali. It is about a third of the way up the western side of the sacred mountain, Gunung Agung. We got there at noon. At three thousand feet up the air was noticeably cooler than at the seaside we had come from. And it was raining, the only rain I experienced in Bali.

Even on the sunniest day Besakih is likely to disappoint anyone who comes looking forward to an ornate temple: they will like the temple at Mengwi much better, and it is much nearer. Yet I felt there was a special sort of atmosphere to misty Besakih with its austere great gate and its black towers rising roof upon roof, and there were so many of them, these thatched pagodas called *meru* (from *Mahameru*, the name of the highest home of the Hindu gods).

29

If the curtain of cloud had risen the ten-thousand-foot mountain Gunung Agung would have been revealed. I had not yet seen the mighty Agung. But the mark of its 1963 eruption was to be seen at the river at the town of Klungkung we had passed through. The river had flowed lava. A slow stream of molten rock just took the bridge that used to span the river and pushed it down to the sea.

The river was wider and shallower than it used to be. From the long bridge that crosses it now people could be seen washing themselves. Women were momentarily bare-breasted, but they managed their sarongs very modestly. They let the wet batik cottons dry on their bodies when they came out of the river, not using towels—which they had; these they used as skull padding so they could carry things on their heads more comfortably.

North of Klungkung, round a place called Bukit Djambul, are rice terraces that my guide, Ngurah, said were the best in Bali. From where we stopped the car on a hilltop and looked down across the terraces, the near ones had just been planted and the pattern was pricked green with the seedling shoots coming out of the irrigation water that reflections glazed with subtle pastel colours. Most of the terraces were water-filled, without any growth as yet. They mirrored sky and clouds and a few palms standing on one of the beautifully irregular lines of the withholding walls that made a stair-like progression of flooded fields right up the hillside.

"THE BEST PLACE for you to eat lunch," my guide said as we came back through Klungkung, "is Gianjar, if you do not mind to eat at the roadside stall. Gianjar is famous for rusted pig."

I had roast pig at Gianjar. So did the guide and the driver. We also had some *satés*, spicy grilled meat on skewers of bamboo, and I had some of the palm beer, *tuak*, and a glass of the heady rice spirit, *arak*. The bill for the three of us was 410 rupiahs, which was at that time one U.S. dollar exactly.

On leaving Rp. 500, I got a big "*Terima kasih, tuan*" ("Thank you, sir") for the tip, and a wide smile from the stall woman, who would have been about fifty and a beauty once. The smile showed she had few teeth left, and those were black from chewing betel-nut. I think Philip Hiss's Balinese, "the happiest people in the world" would be happier if they could afford dentures.

A dog had sat under the trestle table where I lunched, begging with its eyes for scraps, which it got. Ngurah the guide smiled indulgently and said that feeding the dog could start a fight with other dogs that prowled hungrily about. One dirty-white dog was, in part, a husky, the sled-hauler I knew from Greenland, here in the tropical Indies. Ngurah pointed out a brown-and-black dog that is called *blang bungkem* and said it was in demand for sacrificing at crossroads just before the Balinese New Year's Day that falls in our March and is a day of silence when people stay at home and meditate and listen to holy stories and there is no cooking.

Along the road we bought fruit. The taste buds should go on tour, too, and a fine time they can have in South-east Asia with such exotica as—if I may begin with a personal favourite— the *mangosteen*. About the size of a mandarin, it has a rind thicker than and almost as purple as a passionfruit's, and within nestle pearly-white segments of the most delicious citrus-like flavour. Mangosteens should be cheap in January-March, but in the tourist season are less so. And mangoes—one could go on about the sheer sensuousness of mangoes: the shape, the essence-of-the-tropics smell of the skin, and the flavour, like no other, of that brighter-than-golden flesh, a taste so voluptuous that I can't imagine a Cromwell or a Calvin eating a mango. There are a number of mango varieties. Bali has the sweetest—but the tourist season is not the mango season. Common in Bali during the tourist time is the small *rambutan*, red and hairy on the outside, its sweetness packed round a loquat-sized stone. The spiky green *zursak* is full of juice that also sells as a bottled soft drink. The pomelo, called *djeruk bali*, is between a grapefruit and a mandarin, and makes a citrus drink. *Belimbing,* sometimes "starfruit", I have squeezed into gin instead of limes; but limes are better than this aciduous thin sweetness. *Salak* has the look of a chestnut upholstered in snakeskin, and its taste is loquat-like. *Jackfruit* is large, golden-brown and goose-pimpled, with a taste less memorable than the sweeter-than-sweet deliciousness— and foul smell like rotten onions—of the large and spiky *durian*.

31

Ordinarily, hotels won't serve durian because of its odour. But its creamy flesh is a taste experience, even though eating durian is burp-making.

KINTAMANI is as far as short-stay visitors are likely to go from Sanur (or from Denpasar if they stay in Denpasar, and I can see no good reason why anyone should stay there, away from the sea breeze in this unremarkable and rather ugly town). Five thousand feet up, higher than Besakih, Kintamani is also farther off, forty-odd miles.

It is in the northern half of the island, which is not so much visited now that people fly direct to Denpasar instead of coming across the strait from Java to Singaradja. Rarely does a tourist go to the western part of Bali, which is relatively arid and unattractive. However, Negara is said to be worth visiting when the bull races are being held. The "bulls" are water-buffaloes and they are raced in pairs. If there are any tigers left on Bali, the dusty hills of the island's wild west are where they roam. The southern appendage, below the isthmus where the airport is located, is a harsh tableland of limestone. Bali is beautiful, but only in parts.

On the way to Kintamani you come to Tampaksiring, place of the holy springs. The water that bubbles out of the ground fills large baths through decorative stone spouts, and the Balinese believe there is great virtue in bathing here: the waters purify and cure. Outside the temple a notice in English says: "It is prohibited to enter without decent dress and for women having menstruation." As a sign of respect a scarf needs to be worn, round the waist, when you enter a temple's gate. At Tampaksiring scarves can be hired for a small sum.

The temple is known to have been there a thousand years. It was much renovated and partly rebuilt in 1969; but lichens have rooted in the soft stone, weeds have sprung from crevices and moss has spread an ageing green so that the look of new construction has quite gone. Here at Tampaksiring the Hinduism we associate with India rears such forms as the sacred *naga* serpents carved in stone either side of the turtle that bears the world on its back, and the bull of Shiva, and the phallic symbol of the *lingam*.

32

Nothing could be less congruous with this temple scene than what you see when you look up to the crown of the hill above Tampaksiring. Along it stretches the contemporary architecture of the expensive summer palace that was built for ex-president Sukarno.

We go on to Penelokan, which means the "looking place". The view is across a great volcanic basin in which Gunung (Mount) Batur rises to 5,600 feet, and beside it lies Lake Batur. On the far side of the lake is a village called Trunjan, seldom visited by tourists; but I could have joined a party of Australian art teachers who had got up at five o'clock that morning to go to it, crossing the lake in a hollow-log boat. Trunjan is a *Bali Aga* (original Balinese) village, primitively conservative. I had been put off Bali Aga villages by what the painter Donald Friend said about another of them, Tenganan: "This place is like an ingrowing toenail."[8]

Arrived at Penelokan, I am looking across the valley at a plume of smoke drifting from what is evidently a small crater on the side of Gunung Batur. Suddenly there is a big spurt of smoke that billows up, and a noise like a train crossing an iron bridge. About five minutes later this happens again, and it goes on happening at five-minute intervals.

Batur erupted in 1917, violently and with earthquakes, killing hundreds of people in the valley, where there was a village. The lava flow stopped at the gate of its temple. The villagers took this as a sign from the gods that where the temple remained so could they. In 1926 the mountain erupted again, and this time it buried temple and all. So the villagers moved to the high ground the road runs through, and they set up a new temple there. I went into its complex of gateways and *meru* pagodas and shrines. Most of the guardian demons on the gateway had only been rough-cut in the grey stone, giving an odd effect of cubist sculpture. The carvers would finish them, as is usually done, on the site, when the village could afford this.

At Kintamani I joined for lunch Mr Lie of Golden Bali Tours and the amiable proprietors of Segara Village Hotel I was moving to, Ida Bagus Kompiang and his wife. The table was outside what used to be the house of a German artist and is now a small hotel, Wisma Pelni, with only three guest rooms, four beds in each. This was perched on the edge of the deep valley and the dramatic view was across to Batur. Closer than it had been at Penelokan was the mountainside crater that regularly exploded smoke and noise. Once it thundered quite loudly and put up a passable imitation of an atomic mushroom cloud.

To Batur and a farther mountain, Abang, there was a backdrop of clouds. Once, and only for a moment, the clouds parted and I glimpsed the enormous nakedness of Gunung Agung, towering as high again as we were at Kintamani, where the air was like iced hock to the coast's tepid water and, although the sunlight was as bright as a blade, Mrs Astuty Kompiang had put a cardigan across her shoulders.

NORTH OF BEDULU, where the very good Puri Suling restaurant was, I must have passed through, on the way to Tampaksiring, the village of Pedjeng. Oddly, the guide did not mention—and five out of seven books I have read on Bali do not mention— what I missed seeing at Pedjeng. In the temple there is a remarkable drum. It is called the "Moon of Pedjeng".

Covarrubias wrote of this drum as being "perhaps the most remarkable of antiquities in Bali"[2] and there is reference to it, and an excellent photograph of part of its decoration, in the *Guide to Bali*.

It has been dated back to 300 B.C. But Sir Robert Blackwood, who has some standing as an archaeologist, obviously doesn't believe that dating and says, "The drum certainly dates from the ninth century".[6]

The drum is of bronze and is described as shaped like an hour-glass and over six feet long, and it is said to be the largest drum in the world cast in a single piece. It is regarded as sacred and kept in a high place in a pavilion of the Panataran Susih temple (*susih* means moon). The story is that one of the moons in the sky—a different moon was supposed to appear each month—fell down. It was caught in a tree and hung there giving off a light so bright that thieves couldn't steal anything because there was no cover of darkness. Bent on extinguishing the light, one thief climbed up and urinated on the fallen moon, which exploded, killing the thief, and it fell to the ground in the form of this drum that is broken at the base.

34

The sides of the drum are decorated with eight stylized faces in low relief. They are longish faces with very large round staring eyes, not at all Chinese-looking, but "strongly Indonesian" Covarrubias decided, even though the drum was "of the style of so-called drums of the Han dynasty [202 B.C.— A.D. 221] often found in Indo-China and even in Java, but it is the largest and most beautiful I have ever seen."[2]

This Pedjeng drum had been linked with the Dong-son bronze culture, so called from finds of drums at Dong-son in what is now Vietnam. It is a culture thought to have penetrated down from China into South-east Asia perhaps as early as 600 B.C. and not later than 300 B.C.

A stone casting mould for a similar type of drum has been found in Bali, according to the *Guide to Bali*, and this "proves that a highly sophisticated technique of bronze casting was used by ancient Indonesians".[7]

THE MONKEY FOREST of Sangeh is straight north of Denpasar about an hour by car and is best visited as an afternoon run that returns by a rural road that comes to a former *radja's* seat with an elaborate temple and goes on to peter out at the seaside, where the sunset scene is all the better for a theatrical small temple standing high above the waves.

On the way to Sangeh rice was being harvested picturesquely by a coloured line of people in variegated dress, men and women, advancing through the tawny crop and cutting it with small sickle-knives. Then there was an old man tying the rice into bundles that could be carried at either end of a shoulder pole. And, as though to complete the cycle of what happened to the rice, there were two young women pounding the grain into rice flour. This they did in what was like an outsized stone mortar. The pestle was a pole of wood they thumped in, letting go of it as they did so, and it bounced back into the hand. They were doing this bare-breasted. When they saw my camera they turned, and laughed back over their shoulders. A pity they have become self-conscious, because they were particularly comely.

Along the ridges between sections of ricefield, boys who looked not older than six or seven were cutting the grass. You

35

wondered why they weren't in school, then remembered that school was only in the morning. There always seemed to be plenty of children about with their big grins and their "Ullo! Ullo!" shouts to any car with a foreign face in it. Even the naked toddlers jigged and beamed.

Adult male behaviour is seldom exaggerated by alcohol, as it so commonly is in our society, because the Balinese are traditionally abstemious. The women's air of self-control and dignity must owe a good deal to the disciplinary practice of carrying things on the head. You can't get emotional—put your nose in the air, shrug a shoulder or cock a derisive hip—while balancing anything from a kerosine-tin of coconuts to a high-piled temple offering. We are left admiring the grace of this carriage, as well as its skill, even when what is being carried is a basket full of stones to repair a pothole in the road. This is because the Balinese figure is as good as it is, slim in the hips, and the grace that would be lost to a broad and rolling bottom is accentuated by the long and form-fitting batik sarong topped with the neat coatee-style blouse they usually wear.

We passed numbers of women working on road repair: they seem to do more of it than men. And you see them on every construction job—the world's comeliest builders' labourers, carrying small baskets of sand on their heads to the mortar mixers, six women doing as much in a day as one strong man could do with the aid of a wheelbarrow. But the builders' attitude seems to be: When female labour is so cheap and plentiful, why buy a wheelbarrow?

Other questions are posed by culture contact, Balinese with ours. Nowadays a woman may be carrying on her head a packed shopping bag made of plastic. We tend to regard this plastic bag as, aesthetically, a misfortune, an eyesore. But to the Balinese woman it is not only functional but admirable, an exotic status symbol, and one of the few such she has ever been able to afford. Are we, then, glad that few Balinese women can afford to buy what they like but we don't?

Then there is the woman tourist who has just come from the hairdressing salon at the Hotel Bali Beach, where she had a shampoo-and-set for three dollars and tipped forty cents. Looking out of the tour car she notices two Balinese women sitting on the steps of a kampong gateway. What are they doing—? *Why, one is picking lice out of the other's hair.*

What are they supposed to do? Leave the lice in? Use a shampoo they can't afford to buy?

THE MONKEYS of the Monkey Forest at Sangeh are, as the guide puts it, "very friendly". What this really means is that they like peanuts, which you buy at the entrance, and the monkeys want them and for as long as you can supply peanuts you can have an entourage of monkeys.

The thing about monkeys is their movement, so swift and sinuous. You feel that, because humans have the edge on them mentally, monkeys are out to make us look physically foolish—musclebound, slow, almost spastic.

The forest the monkeys live in is unusual. The trees are very tall and straight, as straight as telegraph poles. They are *palala*-trees (often called *pala*) and they have short branches and broad leaves that let hardly any light through to the forest floor. A dark wall of pala-trees flanks the road that leads to the small seventeenth-century temple at Sangeh, a temple on which so little sunlight falls that it has turned green. One sculptured demon was covered completely with moss like green plush. Even the light seems tinged with green.

On the way back we leave the main road and take one that branches to Mengwi, and along this road the Arcadian quality of rural Bali is expressed in long perspectives of thatched mud walls to the kampongs either side; then there are shimmering ricefields, their green becoming gilded in the westering sun; the pale oxen are being brought back to the village; and ducks are gathering to the fluttering wands of the boys who will march them home.

Mengwi was the centre of a principality when Bali consisted of a number of these, each with its *radja* who was like a little king, and was usually in a state of war with one or more of the other radjas. The temple we visit at Mengwi is called a "royal" one and, more elaborate than most, is rich in sculptural ornament.

As well as guardian figures, including Garudas, and faces fanged and glaring, there is a wealth of sheer decoration, carved mainly in the grey stone set in the rosy-red brickwork, but also

37

patterning the wooden doors of shrines. It is an extensive temple complex, and particularly well kept, with an impressive main gateway and a moat right round.

Tanah Lot is a temple of the sea. Where the road ends we look across to a great rock that becomes marooned as an islet when the tide is high; but when the tide is low you can walk across to it, as we did. The temple on the rock is small and a bit decrepit and of no special interest in itself. But the *meru* pagodas it consists of—with a few trees that somehow find soil substance on the rock, which has been deeply undercut by the action of the sea—these silhouette very photogenically at sunset as the whole rock darkens against a chromatic sky.

If you go out to the right of where the road ends, another stretch of scenic coast to the westward comes into view, and there is a near headland that the sea has pierced right through.

The first tour the Bali visitor makes may not be any of the three tours described. It may well be the shorter one that goes to Ubud, by way of Batubulan, Tjeluk and Mas. These places are centres of the arts the next chapter deals with.

"*Everybody is an artist, no?*"

ON THE TOUR I took to Ubud there was a Viennese woman who cocked her head and pursed her lips as she looked at another of the hundred or more Balinese paintings in a gallery in this village and said, to nobody in particular, "In Bali everybody is an artist, no?"

No. But to think that every Balinese is an artist is understandable, especially in Ubud. The village has a number of galleries where Balinese painters display their art, and behind every shop there seems to be a studio. Also there is a notable museum of paintings and carvings at Ubud.

Everybody living in Bali is not necessarily Balinese; and of the five foreigners I met who live there, four were painters. The influence of European artists is what has produced the upsurge in Balinese painting. That and tourism, which provides a market for the pictures—which are quite different from what the Balinese used to paint.

What Balinese painting used to be like tourists will see if they go, as many do, to the town of Klungkung, twenty-five miles north-east from Denpasar. The eighteenth-century Hall of Justice—called the Kerta Gosa, it stands beside an imposing, moated pavilion—has all the undersides of its roof covered with scenes. Some illustrate the story of the *Mahabharata* epic, some depict religious rites, social customs and heavenly rewards for virtue; and those closest to the eye show the torments evil-doers could expect in a Hindu hell, such as flaming torches applied to the genitalia. In 1930 (when the Klungkung "high court" was still operating) painting was "little in evidence as a living art", Covarrubias wrote. The characters depicted were invariably gods, devils, nobles and their retainers, wearing ancient Hindu-Javanese costume. "Painting," he said, "is at a standstill".[2]

The change began in the early thirties. A German painter, Walter Spies, and a Dutch one, Rudolf Bonnet, handed out Western art materials, wondering how the Balinese would use these. Taking their cue from the Europeans, the Balinese began to paint for the first time the things of their own environment—ricefields, festivals, people bathing in streams, the tropical landscape—instead of the traditional subject matter of religious mythology. The scenes produced were lushly detailed and decorative. But, says one writer who saw in the elongated figures the influence of Spies's style, in this manner of painting there is "a kind of ladylike refinement that is its weakness".[9]

A more recent development is called the Young Artists School. This was nurtured by Arie Smit, a painter who came from Holland in 1939 (as a Japanese prisoner-of-war, he helped build the famous bridge over the River Kwai) and has taken Indonesian nationality.

"I didn't let them paint as I do. They needed to paint in their own style and I kept my work away from them," Arie Smit told me at his house in Denpasar. In 1959 he saw a boy of twelve sketching in the sand, and asked him would he like to be shown how to draw on paper and paint with colours. The boy,

39

who was about to quit primary school, said he'd like that; but his father said, "Who will mind the ducks?" Arie Smit lent the money to hire a duck minder. The boy has grown up to be a full-time painter, married with two children, and pupils of his own now.

Just as Australian Aboriginal painters of the Arunta school painted the same kind of Central Australian scenes in the same watercolour style that Albert Namatjira learnt from Rex Battarbee, so the painting of one Balinese "Young Artist" is much like that of another. The style is, compared with what came from the Spies-Bonnet influence, more Balinese, less pseudo-sophisticated and much more colourful, with a strong overall patterning that can be brilliantly decorative. There was an excellent example on the wall of my Inter-Continental hotel room. Sizeable canvases of this kind were on offer at Ubud galleries for as little as twenty-five dollars.

Unlike Western painters, the Balinese have never striven after an individualistic style. In a communal culture there is no copyright. If a festival scene by Wajan Kembang looks very good and proves highly saleable, it is all right for others to paint the same kind of picture in the same way, and not only is it all right ethically but it is essential economically if a young painter is to live by painting instead of, usually, working in his father's ricefield. The father of Njoman Londo, one of the best painters, didn't own a ricefield: he was only a grasscutter. Njoman Londo says unabashedly that his favourite subject is the *Barong* dance, "because it sells the best". He does not want to be a grasscutter.

TOURISTS also go to see, and buy, the paintings of Ubud's two resident non-Balinese artists. Antonio Blanco was born in the Philippines where his Spanish father was a doctor. He is married to a Balinese and has a particularly beautiful daughter. His paintings have flourish and flamboyance, as does the whole Blanco studio-*ménage*. It is beautifully sited on a height where there towers an eleven-tiered pagoda in the thatched *meru* style.

Han Snel came in 1950, as a Dutch Army officer, to fight guerillas. In 1971 I talked to a handsome man of forty-five who referred to himself as a "white Indonesian", introduced a most attractive Balinese wife, and said they had two daughters, nine and ten, who danced *legong*. He also said he would never return to Europe. The place he had made, with its wall-gardens and water-gardens, was much admired by a stream of visiting tourists. Han Snel's art used to be mainly in pastels. The colour-patterned woodblock prints he was doing seemed to me to be better.

The Australian painter living on Bali, Donald Friend, I already knew, and his work I like best. His house at Sanur is beautifully constructed of Balinese materials. Round pillars of coconut-wood rise to a roof that has *lalang* grass tied to bamboo on its underside. Being open to the breeze, as tropical houses need to be, Donald's house is almost as vulnerable as it is lovely, and he has in it a fine collection of Balinese artefacts, some of them bronze and more than two thousand years old.

A carving was stolen. Donald found that in such a case routine police procedure—beating a dozen suspects in the hope of getting one to confess—was not only deplorable but unlikely to produce results: it commonly happened that none of the unfortunate suspects was the guilty party. It was better to call in a magician, a *dukun*. This he did after a small boy of his household—who used to polish the stolen carving and knew it well—spotted it on a shelf in a Denpasar antique shop. The *dukun* somehow produced the name of the thief who sold it to the shop. He belonged to an inland village, but wasn't there. But people have to come back to their village every seven months* for the birthday of the temple. The thief came back and the waiting police nabbed him, and recovered another carving he had stolen from someone else.

There were NO ADMITTANCE signs at Donald Friend's place and a notice that visitors would be seen only by appointment, which was difficult to make since the artist declined to have a telephone. He had two watchmen to preserve his privacy and guard the place. Neither was to be seen when I came one night, and Donald was not at home. When I returned next morning, he said he had come home to find his watchmen had taken the evening off and gone to a dance in a near village.

* The Balinese year is only 210 days long.

41

I asked, "What do you do in a case like that?" and Donald Friend said, "What you *don't* do, with Balinese, is lose your temper and scream at them."

On discovering that the watchmen were missing, he had piled up their bicycles, some chairs and logs of wood into a barricade across the entrance. Then he went to bed. In the morning the barricade had been dismantled, and nothing was said. But they had "got the message". Just as the cook and his boy had when Donald found the kitchen dirty. He simply took the garbage cans and emptied them in the middle of the floor. This proved much more effective than yelling, "The place is like a pigsty!"

A Balinese artist whose talent was spotted by Donald Friend was Ida Bagus Njoman Rai, who worked in a pavilion annexe of the house and did monotone paintings that Donald sent abroad and sold for him. (Two of Rai's scenes are reproduced as endpapers to this book.) The Ida Bagus prefix to his name indicates that he is of the high Brahmana caste: it means "high-born and beautiful". A first son will bear one of three forenames, Wajan, Putu or Gde. A second son is commonly Madé. Njoman simply means third son.

Family planning is "in" and many Balinese women are being given the IUD loop. Sukarno, when he was president, did not approve of birth control. One of his chauvinistic convictions was that Java alone, although it had to import rice, could support a population of 120 million.

Sex doesn't appear to rear much of a head on the Bali scene. As against the statement I read that virginity after puberty was "practically unknown", more than one Balinese guide I talked to maintained that most girls of nineteen—the age when they commonly get married—were virgins. Separation of the sexes before marriage is traditional, although it is breaking down in Denpasar. In the villages you don't see boy-girl togetherness, and never a young couple holding hands—although it is all right for men to do that. Male hand-holding might suggest a high incidence of homosexuality; but that is not at all the case, I was assured. "Playing around" between adolescent males was not considered uncommon, my informants said; but exclusive homosexuality in males, such as is not unusual in Western society, is in Bali virtually unknown.

Prostitution, rampant in just about every other Asian place outside Communist China, may well appear to the visitor not to exist in Bali. It does, of course. But one guide told me that some Japanese male tourists—whom he considered excessively randy—had, after returning from a small hotel brothel in Denpasar, complained that Bali was "not a good place for girls". The guide said that the girls available were much less likely to be Balinese than importees from Java.

Two BOYS, aged about twelve and fourteen, were earning a hundred rupiahs, say twenty-five cents, a day for the work I watched them doing at the village of Batubulan. They were sculptors.

They were carving demons such as serve as guardians at family shrines, or add Balinese atmosphere in the grounds of tourist hotels. There are a couple of big fierce-faced ones at a roundabout intersection in Denpasar to scare off the evil spirits that cause traffic accidents. One boy carver, gouging the stone with a chisel, was putting the finishing touches to eyeballs that bulged out of a visage that was livid in pale grey stone.

The stone the boys were cutting is a siltstone formed of compacted volcanic ash. It is almost the only stone there is on Bali, which is devoid of mineral-bearing rocks, and it is taken from the banks of rivers. This grey stone's being rather soft has two results. The sculptors have no difficulty in carving it into all the baroque and florid forms beloved of Hindu art. And the carvings don't last for centuries; they have to be renewed. So the sculptors are for ever sculpting, and the figures they carve don't change; they are the same old fierce and fangy policemen from the Hindu pantheon.

One writer on Bali, in doing his obligatory worry about the effects of tourism, suggests that among Balinese artists the sculptors are "least affected by the growing commercialization of the arts" because temple gates will not fit into tourist suitcases. Actually, it would be no bad thing if a sculptor-type Arie Smit spearheaded a break with the hidebound forms that must be about as creatively exciting for a Balinese sculptor to do as it would be for a stone carver in Athens to turn out yet another Discus Thrower. The boys I saw carving, remarkable as craftsmen, could quite possibly become artists.

I inquired what a four-foot-high figure such as they were working on would cost, and my guide said about 5,000 rupiahs, less than $12. Which is absurdly cheap, and still would be if it cost as much again to ship it home. But who in Sydney, San Francisco or Southampton wants an apoplectic- and overdressed-looking stone ugly guarding the garden path with an upraised club?

WOODCARVINGS from Bali have gone into thousands of tourist suitcases since the 1930s when the present souvenir-style carving began. Before that just about all carved wood was for use—as doors, pillars, bed-ends, stands for gamelan instruments, masks, kris handles—or for religious ritual. Much carving was ornament, some of it nearly as curly and convoluted as the Chinese. Nearly all of it was painted or gilded. (Natural wood is "new".) Apart from the *radjas*, there weren't many rich to buy this kind of carving. So there were not many carvers. With the wealth of the nobility diminished first by the Dutch and then by the Indonesian government, there would be few carvers today in Bali if it were not for the tourist-souvenir and foreign-export markets.

Now there are a great many woodcarvers, a hundred of them in one village, Mas. This has come of carving figurines, such as elongated young women, nicely breasted; very old men, also attenuated, and so deeply wrinkled that people exclaim over the craftsmanship of carving so much expression of age into the faces; and the boy on the water buffalo. It would be unfair to say that there are no Balinese *objets d'art* on offer more imaginative than these popular pieces; and it must be acknowledged that the craftsmanship is good, the finish meticulous, and the polished wood attractive—the teak, the blond jackwood, the beautiful dark red *sawo*, coconut-wood with its curious texture, and ebony imported from the Celebes. But I did not buy anything.

Twenty years ago I might have. The fact that I don't want it

BALI

Right:
*Children at a
temple festival
get their "sweets"
on banana leaf.*

*A priest helps
women decorate
Kehen temple for
its festival.*

Author's Ektachromes

Below:
*Brilliantly decorative
are the arrangements
of fruits, cakes
and confections
women bring to
offer to the gods.*

Ektachrome by Koes/Bali

Overleaf:
*Women in a long procession mount the steps leading up to Kehen temple,
balancing their high-piled offerings on their heads with grace and skill.*

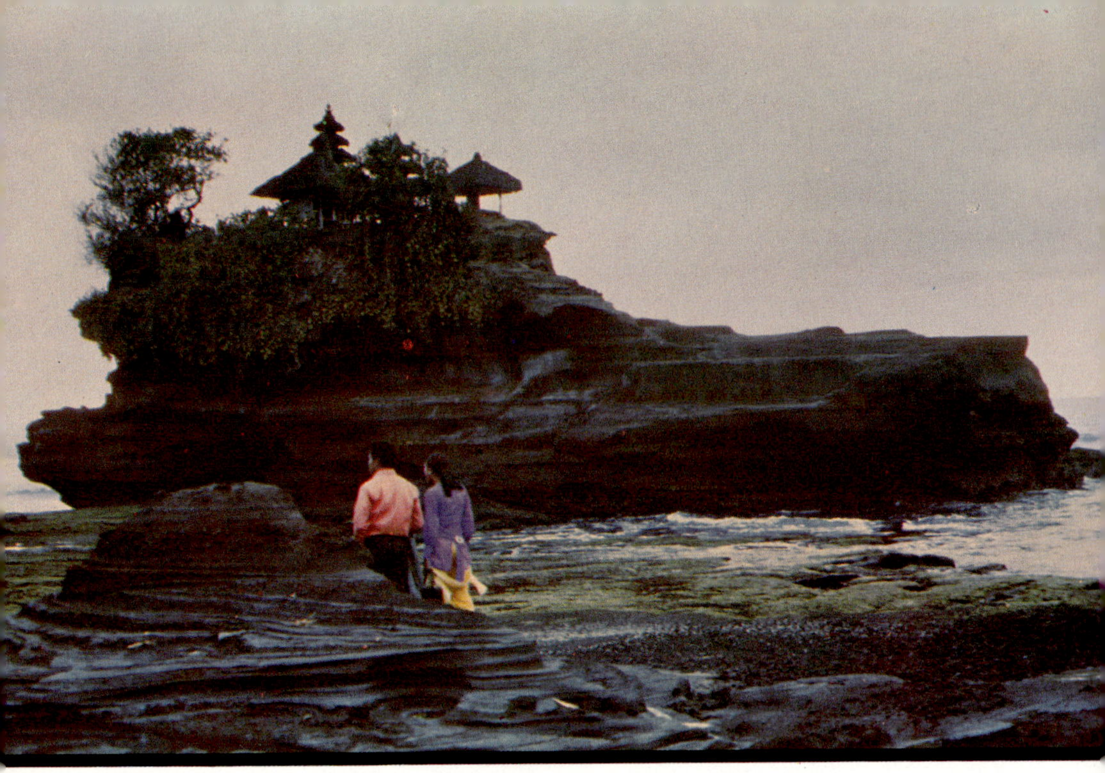

Tanah Lot is a small temple atop a great rock that at high tide is marooned as an islet off the south coast of Bali. It is specially picturesque at evening.

BALI

Author's Ektachromes

At Tampaksiring a shrine is guarded by decoratively carved Nagas (god-snakes) of Hindu mythology. Bali is the only Hindu part of Indonesia.

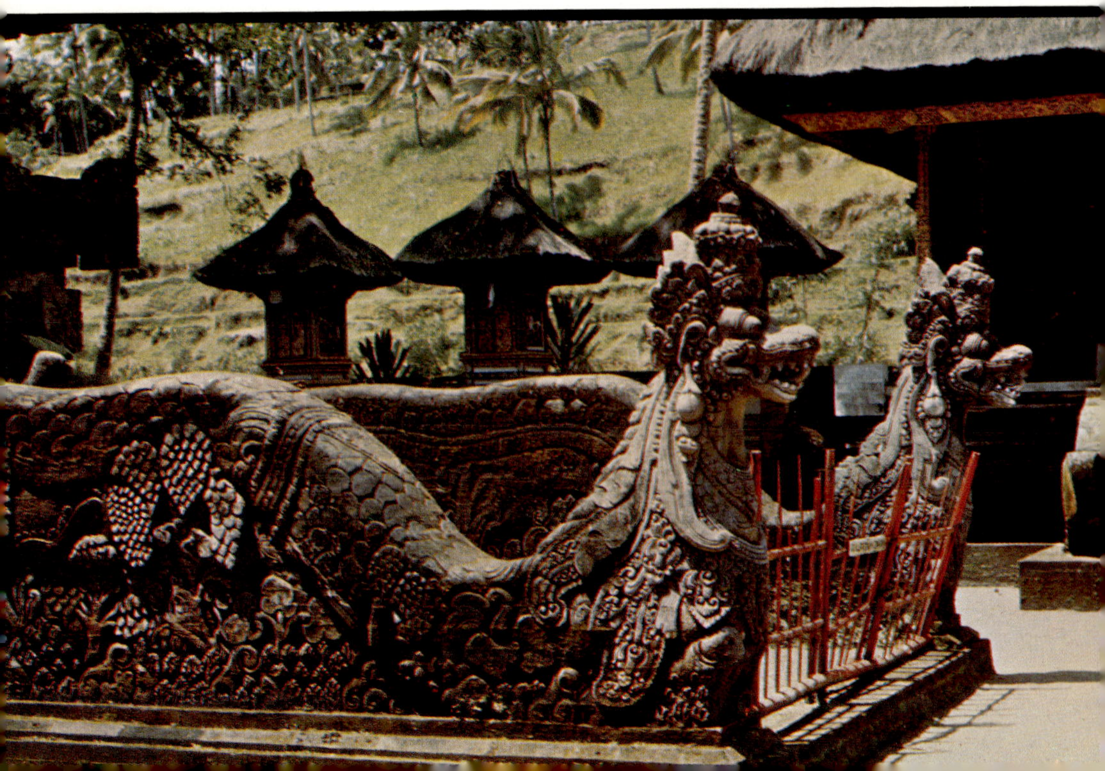

does not mean that I have come to think of all Balinese wood carving as *kitch*. It is what it is. And I do not agree with those who infer that, but for the "tourist commercialization", these Balinese woodcarvers would be carving more aesthetically. They wouldn't be carving at all; they would be squelching behind the ox-plough in the ricefield, or the younger ones would be duckherds and grasscutters, and some would doubtless be labourers in Denpasar.

Better to be one of the twenty or thirty carvers sitting on the matting of a pavilion at the Mas art factory of Ida Bagus Tilem; or one of the polishers, even, shining up the teak with Kiwi boot polish. Ida Bagus Tilem has the well-fed look of a successful businessman, but he also has the reputation of being a notable carver, his father's son: Ida Bagus Njana, in his sixties, was reputedly the best carver in Bali. One of his wood sculptures sold in America for $5,000 and his work was exhibited at the New York World's Fair in 1961.

Ida Bagus Njana was not in his *balé*, his pavilion with a huge carved four-poster bed in it, when I was at Mas. His son said he was making his reverences at the temple, which had an ornate gate in the split style, of warm red brick with grey stone sculptural decoration. In the showroom I saw some of the old man's work. It was not in the Balinese tradition any more than it was in the new souvenir style. It was much more imaginative and used distortion to gain its effect, which is legitimate enough. Some of it seemed to me to have the kind of vigour and volume to its forms that looks so right in Eskimo art, but doesn't belong with the Balinese ethos.

Another famous carver, Tjokot, lived in the off-track village of Djati that you can get only part-way to by car from Ubud. Tjokot was reputedly aged ninety and losing his sight. He took tree-trunks—or a whole section of a tree with a limb or two attached to the trunk—and carved them into spirit figures, the animistic forms of supernatural potencies the Balinese believed in before they got the Hindu gods from India.

There was a tree trunk thus carved (I don't know if it was by Tjokot or one of his carver sons or by an imitator of his style) at the Segara Village Hotel, in a very light wood, and I thought highly of it. American collectors have been acquiring Tjokot's pieces as well as Njana's and Tilem's. Sir Robert Blackwood writes of Balinese carvers as "the world's finest craftsmen in wood".[6]

There was also carving in bone, cowbone that tourists sometimes mistook for ivory—until they heard the price for the intricately carved ornament they were offered: usually two dollars. Which could be, and often was, bargained down to one dollar.

BATIK is everyday wear for Balinese, at least from the hips down. Batiks galore are displayed in the shops of Denpasar and in the roadside vendors' stalls—but Bali doesn't make any batik, or hardly any. Nearly all you see there is made in Java, at Jogjakarta and Solo, and the traveller who is going to those places can buy batiks cheaper there.

However, if the idea is to have the material made up into dresses or shirts, Bali may well be the only place where the stay is long enough for this to be done. A shop named Popiler in Denpasar that was recommended to me did a good job of making two batik leisure shirts.

Brocades are woven in Bali and they glitter with threads of gilt and silver. Less ornate but very colourful, in a checkered pattern, was the kind of weaving done at Batuan village, which is noted for its woven cotton scarves and sarongs.

Jewellery-making centres on the village of Tjeluk. Gold and silver filigree work can be bought for considerably less than we are asked at home after import duty and a higher profit margin have been added.

What some people find interesting—and these are now antiques, in their way—are *lontar* books. The old Balinese way of making a book was to scratch writing and drawing on a dried leaf of *lontar* palm with a fine point of iron. The leaf was then rubbed over with a mixture of soot and oil: this filled each scratch and left it defined as a thin black line. The "pages" were then enclosed within covers made of slices of bamboo, and held in place by a string passed through a hole in the centre of each leaf. To the ends of this string that tie the book closed are usually attached old Chinese coins with the square hole through them, which used to be Balinese currency.

The Hindu "scriptures", priestly literature and instructions for working magic, were all written on *lontar* books. The one I got at Klungkung was nine inches long by less than two inches wide—they are commonly of this shape—and did not cost much more than a dollar. There is drawing on one side of the leaf and writing on the other. The story, the guide said, is from the *Ramayana*, and it is illustrated, strip-style, in a lively manner of sketching.

THE SHADOW PLAY, *wayang kulit*, is the great storyteller of Balinese village life. It uses puppets that are flat, cut out of leather, cowhide. The puppeteer, the *dalang*, tells the story, which is usually from the *Ramayana* or the other epic the *Mahabharata* (War of the Bharatas), a sort of Indian *Iliad*. The *dalang* also provides the sound-effects, and there are accompanying musicians with gamelan instruments. The puppeteer sits behind a screen. The light is always the flame from an oil lamp: even where electricity is available it is not used, because there is a certain dramatic quality to the flicker and glow of the oil flame.

For the visitor *wayang kulit* is dubiously worth hearing, because we cannot understand what is being said; but anyone interested in the graphic arts will find it worth seeing, for half an hour, anyway. The shadow shapes are so decorative, for the leather is cut to produce much more than a simple silhouette. Details of bodies and faces are delineated by lace-like cutting and piercing of the leather, and the rich design of a prince's headdress, say, is patterned in pinpoints of light. The arms of the puppets are movable and, in some, the lower jaw. The bad characters are always on the left side of the screen, the good ones on the right. A stylized tree is most of the scenery.

I was able to go behind the screen and watch the puppeteer at work. Although the audience sees them only as shadows, the leather figures the *dalang* was manipulating were painted. Each one is fastened to a pointed stick and if the puppeteer wants that figure to remain on the screen he jabs the stick into a length of banana-palm trunk that lies in front of him, and is soft enough for this purpose. He sits on the floor of a small pavilion and handles his puppets quickly and so that the action is continuous.

The figures, in the order he will require them, are stacked in a box on his left side. Some, of course, will reappear in the story and must be ready to the hands that manipulate from a low position so that their shadows are not cast on the screen. All the time, he is telling the story—sometimes improvising a humorous sequence—and punctuating it with sound effects. Thwacks of blows he makes with his foot, thumping a box with a beater held between his toes. A *dalang's* is a most demanding job—and it is one that gives him considerable status with the villagers.

"To the Balinese [Covarrubias wrote] the *wayang* is more than vague shadows on a screen. It is the medium for their classic poetry, for their ribald humour; and most important of all, it is the greatest factor in the spiritual education of the masses. . . . Years of training, a thorough knowledge of the stories and their moral value are required of a good dalang. . . . He is invariably the star of the show."[2]

The *wayang kulit* I saw was a performance to which tourists could go, at the village of Kesiman close to Denpasar, at six-thirty in the evening. It lasted an hour.

Of food and festivals

TWO AND A HALF MILLION Balinese live in an island of some two thousand square miles, which is equivalent to no more than a square of land with sides 46 miles long. Much of the island is mountainous and virtually uninhabited; yet, where most of the people live, there does not appear to be the density of occupation we see in the outer suburbs of our cities.

There may be more people to the square mile in Bali but there are fewer structures. Not only are our dwellings larger, but we live with such a spread of facilities and manufactures, with far more shops, with railway stations and bus depots and car service stations and a much greater acreage occupied by schools, hospitals, cinemas and the like. We live large, the Balinese live small.

The average Balinese income-earner made about $20 (under £9 stg) a month, say five dollars a week. Tourist guides were paid $30 a month, and gratuities would have brought this to $50, perhaps more. For taking two people on a full-day, car-with-driver tour that cost $30, the guide commonly got a tip of at least two dollars. Tourist guiding was creamy employment in Bali or anywhere in Indonesia, a much-sought-after job. Qualifications went beyond proficiency in English, a knowledge of history and a likeable disposition. Guides had usually been to university. One of mine was a Bachelor of Arts, another had a degree in Economics. A third I talked to was a graduate in Archaeology.

Another was only a "casual", who turned up every morning at the tour operator's office and was taken on when there was more work than the staff guides could handle, at the casual rate of three dollars a day. He and his wife and baby lived on less than a dollar a day, he said. Rice took 40 rupiahs (say ten cents) and rent—they had one room plus bathroom in Denpasar— was 60 cents (say 25 new pence stg) a week. He could have lived for less in his village, he said. But being highly educated, or relatively so, he did not want to live in his village.

I went through the Denpasar market where this guide's wife shopped for most of what they ate: the meat, when they could afford it, that the vendor wrapped in banana leaf; the rice; the green vegetables; the fruits and flavouring spices. It was a colourful place and aromatic with all the smells, from dried fish to incense. You could buy anything from a clay pot to a fighting cricket, and the market was the place to stretch the buying power of a 100-rupiah note, which was worth less than 25 cents; but to a Balinese it meant more than a dollar means to us.

"They live on three dollars a day," I was told, of the so-called hippies, many of whom were not opt-out hippies at all, but simply long-haired young people seeing the world adventurously in the cheapest way they could. They were down at Kuta beach, where they rented *balés* from villagers to sleep in and got their food from the local stalls.

Some managed to get round the island on hired Honda motorcycles. And the *bemo*, the minibus, was very cheap (25 rupiahs, six cents, for the four miles from Denpasar to Sanur).

There were also a few pony-carts called *dokars*, if you could bear to be hauled by horses that usually looked miserably underfed. Taxis were fairly plentiful, but relatively expensive.

Kuta, six miles from Denpasar, was a better beach than Sanur. The water was deeper, not so reef-strewn, and there was surf. It was on the western side of the isthmus, which meant that it didn't get the refreshing south-east breeze off the sea that cooled Sanur.

When I went to swim there I looked at the hotel accommodation, which was right at the beach. The Kuta Beach Hotel, run by Natour, the national tourist hotel organization, offered very basic rooms, with no air-conditioning or hot water but with dipper bath, for $9 single, $13 double, including breakfast and tax. Much more grand was the new-in-1971 Kartika Plaza resort with rows of brick one- or two-room bungalows, thatched in the Balinese style; air-conditioned and with bathrooms and hot water, well furnished and carpeted wall to wall. The rate for a beachfronting double was U.S. $18 (at the back $16) plus 21 per cent service charge and tax. The beach stretched for miles along a palmy shore. West-facing Kuta was the place to see sunsets.

The Segara Village Hotel I stayed at after a week at the Bali Beach was probably the best medium-priced place, with a very pleasant atmosphere. It did not have air-conditioning or hot-water service then, but it has now; and its bungalow-style accommodation was being extended, so that it was expected to have twenty extra rooms before the end of 1972. Some of the extra bungalows were to be in the distinctive and picturesque style of the Balinese rice-barn, two-storeyed with the thatched roof in half-oval shape. What I had for $12, a day (single), without air-conditioning, hot water and soft mattresses, would probably be $17 a day, but not higher, the proprietor, Ida Bagus Kompiang, said. The special charm of the place was its courtyard garden, with a carp pool and a shrine that always had its daily offering of flowers, and splashes of colour from ceremonial umbrellas and bougainvillaea and crotons. The dining tables were set out in the dappled shade of two big trees; where birds called *betjitja* and *tjruktjuk* made noises like their names.

The hotel was about two hundred yards from the beach at

what is called Segara Beach Market. (*Segara* means "sea".) As was the case at the Hotel Bali Beach (which had its big swimming-pool) and Tanjung Sari, sea bathing was possible only at high tide and even then there wasn't much depth and the bottom was too coralline for comfort and you were advised to wear sandshoes. On the beach you were sure to be besieged by souvenir sellers, children mostly, with cowbone carvings, wooden owls, shell necklaces, as well as old-style painting scrolls and lengths of cloth. They waited for any strollers who came down from the Hotel Bali Beach, where the vendors were forbidden the grounds and the beachfront.

Another beach itinerant, at night, was the massage man. He carried his bottle of oil in his hand and, in fact, gave an excellent massage. He also touted for ten-dollar girls in Denpasar.

The air traveller, having brought in from his flight all the liquor and cigarettes allowable, rather expects to have to pay steep prices when his supply runs out. But no: although Bali is not at all duty-free, I found that Scotch and cigarettes by the carton were available at a Denpasar store at less than Australian prices. They were, I was told, smuggled.

BALINESE FOOD is Indonesian food and Indonesian food is akin to Indian and, to some extent, Chinese food, but closer to Indian because of its spiciness. However, the dish the Balinese are fondest of is roast suckling pig, *babi guling*. Another favourite is *betutu bebek*, duckling roasted in banana leaf.

Nasi goreng is the best-known of Indonesian dishes—unless that distinction belongs to the Dutch-originated *rijsttafel* (rice-table) that consists of so many little dishes that, it has been said, the food gets cold while you're deciding which one to have next. *Nasi* is steamed rice, which is smothered in just about every flavour from onion to chili and served with sautéed beef and chicken legs and a fried egg on top (and some recipes add sliced omelette for good measure). For this dish you need to be hungry.

Bakmi goreng does it with Chinese noodles instead of rice, and without the fried egg. Indonesian boiled chicken (*opor ajam*) is cooked in sweetened coconut milk. An excellent dish I had at the main restaurant of the Hotel Bali Beach, the Raja Room, was *gulai kambing*, cubed lamb done with spices. With most

51

Indonesian food comes a bowl of *sambal*, a sauce made with chillies, and it requires to be treated with caution because it is tongue-bitingly hot.

One of the things I liked best about Indonesian food was the bread—or what you have instead of bread—*krupuk*. This is made of tapioca-flour batter dropped in boiling coconut oil; and it comes out lighter, curlier and softer than Melba toast but still crisp—and tasty. The commonest kind of *krupuk*, pinkish in colour, is lightly flavoured with shrimp.

Good Chinese food was to be had in two Denpasar restaurants named Selera and Puri Selera, in the main street. The less attractive-looking Puri Selera cooked better than the other one where, nevertheless, I had a local fish called *kakap* excellently grilled.

The distinctive Balinese drink is a sweet red rice wine, *brem*. I found it too sweet, and with meals I usually drank beer or iced coconut juice, which is refreshing. Wines, at the Hotel Bali Beach, were expensive to the extent of being about $2.50 for a half bottle of a reasonable claret—but French cost no more than Australian.

Arak is distilled, in Middle East and Far East, from coconut sap, from rice, even from millet, and is so variously flavoured that what is called arak or arrack in Lebanon tastes nothing like the arak of Bali, which is made from coconut sap and has an odd taste that is better than its smell. Not much use was made of arak, except by the enterprising Robert Hargrove who, at his Balinese-style restaurant mentioned earlier, the very attractive Puri Suling at Bedulu, served spiced arak over ice as the "Balinese martini"; and you could also taste arak in his *Ketjak Kooler* a refreshing long drink that had orange juice, *brem* and passion-fruit as well.

TEMPLES in Bali vary a good deal in layout, but if there is a typical one it has a front gate that is "split", as though a mono-lithic structure had been cut down the middle and the two halves drawn apart a couple of feet. This leads to an outer courtyard, and from there a "one-piece" gateway—which is likely to be ornate and have a fearsome guardian's face carved across the lintel—leads to an inner courtyard. Here you probably see a few

52

meru pagoda shrines with black-thatch roofs, but no idols or anything exciting. You may even find yourself counting the *meru* roofs—to check that they are always an odd number, five, seven or eleven, never an even six or ten—because there doesn't seem to be anything else to occupy you. A Balinese temple without a festival going on can be very like a fairground without a fair.

Festivals are many. Not that they happen every week or month at every temple, but there are so many temples within an hour or so's drive of Sanur that the tourist in Bali for a week would be unlucky not to be able to see one.

What makes a temple festival worth seeing is the procession to it of Balinese women carrying the beautifully arranged offerings on their heads. This is something the camera describes better than words can (SEE PLATES). But there were not just the few women pictured: there were hundreds of them. Some I watched setting out a mile down the road from where this temple was. I went ahead by car and when the women reached the temple and had marched up its hundred steps to the top, where I was with camera, some still had their hands at their sides, not even needing to steady the high burdens of fruits and other foods that they balanced on their heads. Their steadiness and control was such that there was the temptation to say, absurdly, that they "moved like statues". And, as well as being so skilful, they were so decorative in their batik *kains* (sarong-like skirts) and bright *kebaja* blouses and sashes. It has been said of the Arabs that they can wear any colour next to any other colour. The Balinese seem to be able to do this with patterns and get away with it.

Balinese religion is not the concern of priests on behalf of the people but of the people themselves. Their beliefs are by no means entirely involved with the gods, but rather more with the spirits of ancestors; and the reverencing of ancestors is a personal thing. As Covarrubias put it: "The main concern of the Balinese centres in the propitiation of the protecting ancestors who descend to this earth on special holidays and at the anniversaries of the innumerable temples, when they receive offerings and entertainment from the people. By these ceremonies and temple festivals the populace hopes to entice the spirits to remain among them; the beauty of the offerings, the pleasant music, the elaborate theatrical performances, aim to keep them from growing bored and leaving."[2]

THE FESTIVAL I saw was at the Kehen temple, the big regional sanctuary at Bangli, which is about thirty miles inland from Sanur. It is a very old temple, the records going back to the beginning of the thirteenth century. And it is a particularly picturesque one, built on a hillside. The steps mount up, past the demonic stone "policemen" standing guard on either side, to a splendrously carved gateway.

Big though this gate is, it and everything else about the temple is dwarfed by an enormous banyan-tree, the largest I have ever seen. A kind of tree-house has been built in it about forty feet up and this houses the *kulkul*, a great wooden gong that is sounded to summon the people or to give an alarm. Part of the inner courtyard the banyan overhangs has a wall inset with coloured plates of Chinese porcelain.

I saw this festival being prepared when we stopped at Bangli on the way back from Kintamani two days before the procession took place. The hard-working priests in their white robes— the *pemangkus*, not the high-caste Brahman *pedandas*— were decorating the shrines so that the spirits would find them attractive to visit. With helpers, they were hanging up *lamaks* (palm leaf beautifully cut into patterns) and, less aesthetically, draping white calico that was boldly stamped with the brand name and proclaimed "BEST QUALITY", even though it cost under 25 cents a yard.

By Saturday all the cane platforms that had been bare were covered with offerings and the *balés* that had been empty were filled with them—or appeared to be, but more and more kept coming in to be lifted off the seemingly endless procession of laden heads and arranged at the many shrines. The courtyard had become kaleidoscopic with the colours of rice cakes and fruits and *lamaks* and sarongs and blouses and the bright clothes of children dressed in their best.

Their offerings placed, the women knelt and, hands together, made their reverences at the shrines their *bandjar* or clan or caste connected them with; but, briefly and without much solemnity.

54

Then they were commingling as on a social rather than a religious occasion. Children ate sweetmeats such as they would at a fair, except that the wrapping was not paper or plastic but a piece of banana leaf. Foodstalls did a busy trade outside. In the outer courtyard a full *gamelan* played, and a dance performance was being readied for later in the evening.

Of the elaborate offerings some would go to the priests; or the roast chicken part might be taken home again or, after it had been offered to the gods, eaten at the festival. The lesser offerings would be left to feed the scavenging dogs and the birds. But, as my guide Ngurah said, "The *essence* of the offerings will go to the gods and the ancestors."

This struck me as being a good arrangement: your gods could have your cake and you could eat it.

A big and happy cremation

"OUR CONCEPT OF DEATH is quite different from yours in the West," Anak Agung Gde Rai explained to me in perfect English. "A cremation, with us, is not a mournful occasion but a joyful one, because the dead person is liberated into the heavenly world."

The dead person in this case was the speaker's father. The Rai family was a noble one, "royal" in its connection with the former *radja* of Bangli. Anak Agung was the title of the young man I had last seen in an immaculate Western suit in his office at the Hotel Bali Beach, where he was Public Relations Manager. Now, at his family house, he was in Balinese sarong and tunic shirt of handsome batik. His role appeared to be less that of chief mourner than of host to hundreds of people at ceremonies in connection with his father's cremation. These had already been going on for two days, and nearly a thousand people had been or would be involved.

The cost of it all, I was to learn later, would be not less than half a million rupiahs, more than $1,000, about £500 stg, or approximately as much as the average Balinese would make in four years. It was a considerable sum for even the Rais to find. Yet it was expected of the family that the cremation ceremonies should be on such a scale.

The Anak Agung Rai's father had died six years before. He was buried, as people usually are, unless they are Brahmana priests, who cannot go in the ground and must be cremated forthwith.

On this third day of the ceremonies the actual cremation was to take place. On Day 1 the "body" had been prepared for the soul's ascent to heaven: the body was symbolized by a small effigy in the form of an engraved tablet of sandalwood, which was placed in a coffin box decorated with coloured paper and topped with a very strange little structure called an *angenan*. This was, in part, a lamp-stand with the lamp made of an egg-shell and symbolizing the soul. The base was a ripe coconut filled with rice, representing the heart.

Day 2 was particularly ceremonious, with everyone in their best attire for the procession to the house of the priest, where the effigy was consecrated. Relatives and friends flocked to the family's shrine to make offerings. Then there was a banquet.

Now it is Day 3 and this morning the Anak Agung went to the cemetery, where the bones of his father were exhumed. He felt "very moved," he tells me, when he took his father's skull from the earth. The bones were cleansed and left at the cemetery. There they will be transferred to the sarcophagus for cremation.

The sarcophagus was by the roadside, outside the walls of the Rai *kampong*, when we arrived. It was in the form of a lion, longer than a real one, and the kapok-tree wood it had been carved from had been painted bright vermilion and given spots and designs in gold. There was a good deal of gold paint on the head with its bulging green eyeballs. From the open mouth a tongue about a foot long curled out between fierce teeth. The lion had a green mane and a rampant tail. It looked like something off a rather beautiful if somewhat barbaric Oriental carousel.

More often the coffin is in the shape of a bull although, strictly the bull was only for the Brahmana caste. An Anak Agung was entitled to a lion. The back was removable, for the

56

bones to be placed inside. The lion stood on a platform that was decorated with a bold floral motif that looked quite gay.

Also ready by the roadside was the cremation tower. In this the corpse, if corpse there had been, would have been borne to the cemetery, and there transferred to the sarcophagus for burning. An ordinary cremation "tower" is less than towering, but this being the *badé* of a nobleman it was elaborate and the top section was like a model of a pagoda, nine roofs high. It was brightly and fancifully decorated with coloured paper and dyed cotton wool, tinsel and tiny mirrors. From the back of the tower base flared the many-coloured face of a beneficent winged monster named Bhoma, who was there to scare off evil spirits.

None of the structure is merely decorative, for it symbolizes the cosmos. The base represents the underworld; the next section, the mountains; the paper flowers, the forests; the pagoda-like roofs, rising above the corpse pavilion, are the heavens; and the ornament at the tip top is the phallic *lingga* of the Supreme Being, whose name is Tintiya.

Word had got round that a big cremation was taking place and a number of people from Sanur's tourist hotels were already there with their cameras. As an invited guest, I could go into the house. I had with me a gift-wrapped package containing the six yards of *kain putih* (white cloth) which it is etiquette to take to a cremation. A great deal, perhaps hundreds of yards, of this material is used. It binds the funeral procession together, and if the corpse is being carried on the tower it connects with the shroud, which is of the same white calico.

We (I had come with my friend Lie of Golden Bali Tours) were served tea in one of the *balé* pavilions that comprised the Rai household. The place looked very gay, and it appeared that there had been some special decoration for the occasion. All the pavilions were full of people, men and women, brightly dressed, and many children, all in their "Sunday best". The Anak Agung took me to the *balé* where his father was, as it were, lying in state symbolically, for the small sandalwood effigy represented his body, as the *angenan* eggshell lamp did his soul.

The soul is believed to be contained in the head. It can come out of the mouth in sleep, and dreams are its wanderings. The soul cannot ascend into Heaven until the body is returned

57

to the elements—air, earth, fire, water—by being burnt and the ashes gathered and taken to a river or the sea.

Cremation, then, to the Balinese is all-important. The soul is withheld from entering heaven for as long as the body's cremation is delayed. Yet *adat* (hallowed custom) decrees that cremation be ceremonized in a manner so costly—the elaborate structures, the payments to priests and for holy water and the obligatory hospitality—that it has to be delayed until people can afford it. Even for the rich there is delay. As for the poor, they commonly cremate *en masse*, twenty-five or so together, and share the expense.

THE PROCESSION to the cemetery was everything from the dignity of a grave-faced girl carrying on her head the *angenan* with the soul's lamp of eggshell—and steadying the precious object with one hand every step of the way—to the wild antics of the sarcophagus bearers.

The bearers of the lion coffin, which was fastened to a platform of bamboo poles, were a dozen barefoot youths in singlets and tucked-up sarongs, and they treated their task with a sort of carnival-air abandon. Not that they did anything that was not always done, traditionally, by the sarcophagus bearers—except, perhaps, when they downed coffin and stood posed with their broadest grins while I took photographs.

Then they were off, and whirling the lion sarcophagus round and round. This is always done to confuse the spirit of the dead one so that he will not return from the cemetery and haunt the family. The fact that the coffin was in this case empty made no difference: it was the best part of being a bearer, this giddying whirl. Moreover, the crowd expected it. So they whirled at intersections and, most vigorously of all, when they left the main road to go into the cemetery.

In the procession there were files of women carrying elaborate offerings—not of food but of decorations done in coloured papers—on their heads; there were bearers of holy-water vessels and ceremonial umbrellas fringed all round; there were brazier carriers perfuming the air with incense; and above all, literally, there was the cremation tower.

The tower, like the sarcophagus, was mounted on a bamboo-pole platform, but a larger one and there looked to be about forty bearers, men who were nearly all naked to the waist and perspiring under their burden. They were carrying three persons as well as the tower—Anak Agung Gde Rai who clung to the tower just below where its pagoda roofs began, another man, and a musician who sat cross-legged and played a *gamelan* xylophone continuously.

More than twenty feet high, the tower approached a calico sign that was hung across the road, exhorting villagers to save their money and put it into government bonds. The tower's designer had allowed for this and hinged the upper portion so that it bent over and cleared the sign. In the same way it went under the telephone wires at the turn-off into the cemetery.

It was all very colourful and strange and one of the watching tourists, a girl with shiny eyes and lots of beads, was moved to remark to the black-bearded young man she was with, "Isn't Bali marvellous? Why even the *dust* smells fragrant!"

"Ah," said the beard, spoiling it, "that's incense."

THE CEMETERY is more like a picnic ground. Except for some Chinese graves with headstones the place has little look of a cemetery, anyway, for the graves of the uncremated have only small markers and are barely distinguishable in the grass that spreads like a rough lawn between the coconut palms and kapok-trees. The drink sellers and food vendors are here and some souvenir sellers have turned up with the tourists. Family parties are settled down on the grass, a cremation being an occasion for a day's outing. The bearers of the cremation tower sit smoking and talking cheerfully and drinking *tuak*, the palm beer.

A secondary, much smaller cremation tower that was not very noticeable in the procession—it contains the sandalwood effigy—is set alight and burns slowly. The big tower will also be burnt, later. The Anak Agung is not in sight and I am told that he has gone to the cemetery's Temple of the Dead, from which he soon returns, with his beautiful wife and relatives and friends, to where we spectators are waiting round a hillock that is now topped with the sarcophagus.

The remains are brought in a white shroud and passed over

59

the heads of the people up to where the lion's back is lifted off like a lid and the bones are placed inside. Now the priests anoint the remains with holy water. Two *pendandas* do this. One is a white-haired old man, his hair done in a topknot: the other is a woman, also with a topknot.

The *mantras* (religio-magical formulas) they are saying are in the ancient Sanscrit language. Their lips move but the words that no one else present would understand are not audible, anyway, because a *gamelan* is playing near by and cicadas are shrilling in the trees. The ritual anointing with holy water goes on until water is running out of the lion's belly and down its legs, and I ask myself how wood so sodden is ever going to burn.

Yet burn it does (aided, I understand, with some rice spirit) and the flames begin to consume the lion. Its mane flares away and its red-and-gold is blackened; the legs become stick-like and the long tongue lolls from a head that remains impressive even when the flame-licked form has become quite skeletal. Smoke curls up between the fronds of the coconut palms. The body that had gone to earth has gone to fire and now to air.

Perhaps the greatest difference between East and West is that while the East continued to reverence the elements the West sought to master them.

CREMATION is by no means the end of the ceremonies. The soul has been liberated, but it has yet to be purified, protected, prayed for and consecrated as a god-spirit with its place in the family shrine. The ordinary Balinese peasant, whose soul is not supposed to go beyond the lowest of the various heaven-levels, anyway, cannot afford much of this ritual; but in the case of high-caste families the post-cremation ceremonies, called *mukur*, are rather like what has already happened happening all over again, after a lapse of forty-two days.

There are more offerings, more feasts, more orchestras hired in and perhaps actors and storytellers, a great deal more ritual involving the priests, and another tower—but this time it is decorated only in white and gold. New effigies are made and burned. Vigils are kept. Finally the ashes are carried in a white-and-gold sarcophagus to the sea or to a river. The fourth element, water, receives the body's remnant. Now there is no

BALI   THE ARTISTS   Author's Ektachromes

Han Snel, shown with his Balinese wife, TOP LEFT, *is from Holland, as is Arie Smit,*
TOP RIGHT, *showing a painting of the colourful Young Artists School, which he fostered.*
ABOVE LEFT, *a boy sculptor at Batubulan and,* RIGHT, *artists at work at Ubud.* BELOW :
The Australian painter Donald Friend in his enviable Balinese house at Sanur.

BALI

"*A cremation with us is a joyful occasion.*"
So, ABOVE, *bearers of the lion coffin pose very
cheerfully and,* BELOW, *a man clowns as he
balances one of the offerings on his head.*

Bearers of the lion coffin whirl it wildy to confuse the spirits. AT LEFT: *For a nobleman the cremation tower is very tall and ornate. A bearer laughs.* BELOW: *At the cemetery the coffin, with bones in it, burns.*

Ektachrome above by S. T. Lie; others by Author.

Close-up of a Bhoma decorating the base of a cremation tower. The purpose of this multi-coloured winged monster is to scare evil spirits away from the ceremonies.
BALI

Ektachromes by Koes/Bali

Wayang kulit (the shadow play) has the puppet characters intricately cut out of water-buffalo leather and stick-manipulated between a screen and an oil lamp's flame.

material barrier to the soul's enjoying celestial bliss—or coming back to earth, newly born into another body.

Call it transmigration of souls or metempsychosis or reincarnation, this is a doctrine that fits very conveniently with the Hindu caste system—if you happen to be high-caste. Belief is that anyone who is low-caste wouldn't be low-caste if he or she had not been sinful in a previous life. Having brought their inferiority upon themselves, they deserve to be in a subservient position. Whereas, if you are of a high caste, you earned your superiority by virtue in a previous existence—otherwise you would not have been born into high-caste family. So your birth attests your superiority.

The feudal nature of Balinese society is indicated in the language. When I talked to the painter Ari Smit I asked him if he spoke Balinese, and he replied, "Yes, but I prefer to speak Indonesian. In Balinese you are supposed to speak in a rough way to an inferior and quite differently to a superior. It is not a sympathetic language. The way we use the democratic 'you' in English in speaking to all classes is incomprehensible to a Balinese, because there is still a large area of the feudal mentality."

Postscript on tourist Bali

A QUESTION being asked after it was announced in August 1972 that cheap air holidays to Singapore would be operated from Australia was whether the air fare was likely to be similarly cut to give low-priced vacations in Bali.

The answer is that this is unlikely to happen before 1974 at the earliest; and it can hardly be said that it is likely to happen then.

A quite different set of circumstances produced the cheap charter-flight holiday to Singapore. There was, for a start, a surplus of hotel accommodation, and Singapore hotel operators were prepared to cut their rates right back to get group occupancies that were marginally economic. In Bali the situation has been the reverse, with the Hotel Bali Beach's only problem being to accommodate all the people who wanted bookings.

Inter-Continental's big hotel will not continue to be the only large luxury-class one on Bali, as it is now. The following were the hotel proposals that had been made for Bali:

–BALI HYATT. The construction contract was let in July 1972 for a 405-room hotel for Hyatt International Corporation, near Denpasar.

–HOTEL BALINESE. This was an Australian project of the Paragon Investment and Development Co. Pty Ltd. Plans show a 600-room resort hotel of striking curved design proposed for the Nusa Dua seaside area.

–TRAVELODGE was considering building in Bali.

–KLM–GARUDA, Dutch-Indonesian airlines, have a hotel site at Sanur for which plans have been prepared.

–LUFTHANSA, the German airline, was reportedly interested in having a German hotel operation on Bali.

–JAPAN AIR LINES were similarly interested in a Japanese resort hotel.

None of the hotel projects mentioned was expected to be built and in operation before 1974.

A proposal to build a Bali Hilton hotel is not being proceeded with.

Central Java

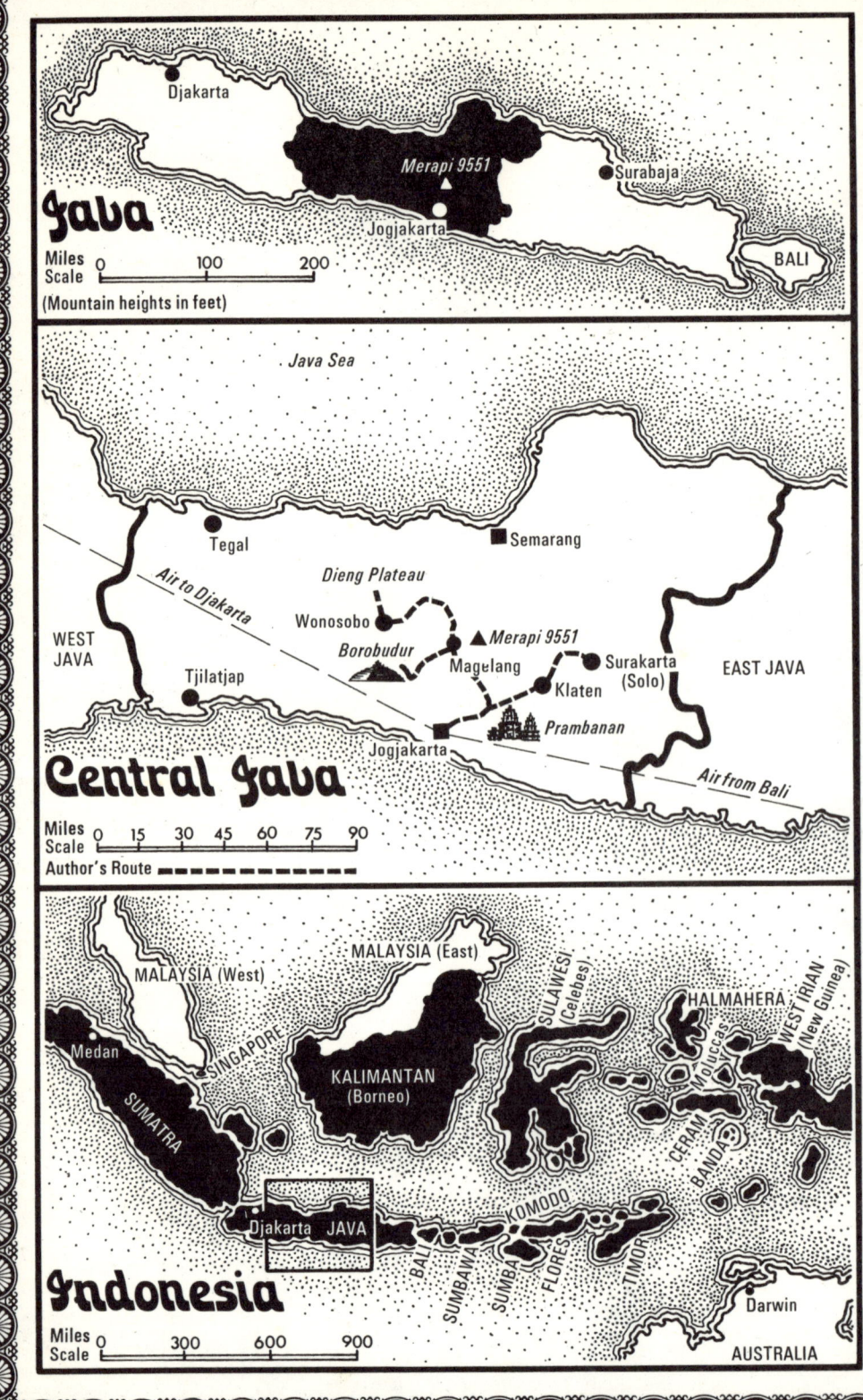

Java

Miles Scale
0   100   200
(Mountain heights in feet)

Djakarta

Merapi 9551

Surabaja

Jogjakarta

BALI

Central Java

Java Sea

Tegal

Semarang

Air to Djakarta

Dieng Plateau

Wonosobo

Borobudur

Magelang

Surakarta (Solo)

WEST JAVA

Tjilatjap

Merapi 9551

Klaten

EAST JAVA

Jogjakarta

Prambanan

Air from Bali

Miles Scale
0 15 30 45 60 75 90

Author's Route ▬ ▬ ▬ ▬ ▬

Indonesia

MALAYSIA (West)

MALAYSIA (East)

SULAWESI (Celebes)

HALMAHERA

WEST IRIAN (New Guinea)

Medan

SINGAPORE

KALIMANTAN (Borneo)

SUMATRA

Moluccas

CERAM

BANDA

Djakarta   JAVA

BALI

SUMBAWA

SUMBA

KOMODO

FLORES

TIMOR

Darwin

Miles Scale
0   300   600   900

AUSTRALIA

Batik country, with monuments

THE PLANE leaving for Jogjakarta in Java is an F28 of the Indonesian airline Garuda. It rises from the Denpasar airport of Bali, the island described in an advertisement of an Australian airline as "the last Garden of Eden". That piece of copywriter's hyperbole is not too surprising, advertising overstatement being the way it is. But raised eyebrows there would be if it were suggested that Bali, or any other part of Indonesia or South-East Asia, was the *first* Garden of Eden.

That kind of claim might be all right in the advertising of a Middle East airline, Iraq's perhaps, because everybody—or everybody who trusts *Genesis* as geography—knows that the Garden of Eden was in the region of the Tigris and Euphrates rivers in what used to be Mesopotamia and, though much of the area is desert now, in ancient times it was the Fertile Crescent.

However, here comes a Pacific-side scholar who puts in a claim for South-East Asia as the cradle of civilization. He is Professor Wilhelm G. Solheim II who heads the Department of Anthropology at the University of Hawaii. According to a proponent of Solheim's theories he ". . . offers the following propositions in suggesting a revision of historical thinking about the region: (i) That the South-East Asians started agriculture long before the people of the Fertile Crescent domesticated plants, (ii) That South-East Asians moulded pottery and bronze much earlier than did either the Indians or the Chinese, (iii)

That the South-East Asian region nurtured a cradle of civilization older than that of the Near East, India or China."[10]

Much more evidence than Solheim has adduced would be required to support these propositions, particularly (iii), which would not necessarily be true if (i) and (ii) were proved to be. The Egyptians did not have bronze (only copper) or the potter's wheel when they built the Great Pyramid around 2,500 B.C., although they had mathematics, writing and a calendar, things that have rather more to do with civilization.

However, Solheim is able to point to archaeological finds that do, indeed, suggest that South-East Asia has been given less than its due. Culturally, it now appears to have been more than a region of peripheral jungle into which enlightenment penetrated from two great clearings called India and China.

Finds made in cave sites at Hoabinh in North Vietnam suggest to Solheim that incipient horticulture may have begun here as long ago as 15,000 B.C. and that this is the area where animals were first domesticated and pottery was first made. Sandstone moulds for the casting of bronze axes, found at Non Nok Tha in northern Thailand, have been dated at between 2,500 and 3,000 B.C. Bronze (alloy of copper and tin) was in use in the Indus Valley civilization in western India by 3,000 B.C., but the earliest evidence of bronze in China is about 1,500 B.C. So it could be that China got pottery from South-East Asia, not vice versa as has long been assumed. Moreover, it also appears from Thai potsherds that glazed pottery went north to China, instead of coming south from it. And the anthropologist Paul K. Benedict avers that words for *plough*, *pottery*, *iron* and *gold* that the Thais were said to have borrowed from the Chinese were, in fact, words the Chinese appropriated from the Thailand region. In South-East Asia, before there was any Indian or Chinese contact, the cultural situation was, Solheim declares, "much higher than anyone had previously accepted".

Even more surprisingly, we may have to revise our ideas of where *Homo sapiens* first came from. Part of a human skull was dug up in the Niah (Great) Cave in Sarawak in 1958, in association with charcoal that was radio-carbon dated as nearly 40,000 years old. As the discoverer, Tom Harrisson, former Curator of the Sarawak Museum, wrote, "Previously, it has widely been

66

concluded that 'modern man' originated much further west, and spread eastward only in later times."[11]

The ethnologist Donald Brothwell, who made an exhaustive study of the skull for the British Museum, concluded from it that "contemporaneous with the later Neanderthal people of Europe and Africa a human type existed in south-east Asia displaying a skull form similar to that of recent Australians and Tasmanians."[12]

The Niah skull was compared by Brothwell to the Australian Aboriginal Talgai skull found in Queensland in 1884, and appeared to be less primitive in type. The Talgai skull has never been considered older than 20,000 years at most, half the possible age of the Niah skull.

WHAT WE KNOW of Indonesian history in eras B.C. is virtually nothing. What we know of it from the beginning of our Christian era up to the coming of the Dutch to these East Indies at the end of the sixteenth century is, compared with what we know of the history of Egypt or Greece, about as a single page is to a tome.

It does appear that Java was still neolithic (New Stone Age), and given to erecting megalithic (big stone) terraced pyramids to the dead, when Hindu culture came in from India about the first century A.D. Indian traders who visited Sumatra were followed by priests, and Hinduism appears to have spread by conversion not by conquest. The religious change from animism seems to have been a very gradual process, with old Indonesian threads patterning the Hindu fabric. The style of Hindu temples owes something to the old megalithic forms. Not that there are any stone temples older than the seventh century A.D.

There was some Buddhism, but not much, in Java in A.D. 414 according to a Chinese pilgrim who wrote in that year. The Buddhist faith, also, came in from India.

Only since 1918, when the French scholar Coedes deciphered old Malay and Sanscrit inscriptions, have we known of the existence of empires of the Javanese Hindu kingdoms of Sri-vijaya (7th-13th century), centred on Sumatra, and Madjapahit (13th-16th century), in East Java. Their influence spread to the Malay peninsula and as far north as the Philippines.

Sri-vijaya kings of the Sailendra dynasty embraced Buddhism and, in central Java about A.D. 800, built the monumental Buddhist temple complex of Borobudur that covers a hill twenty-five miles from Jogjakarta, and we'll come to it.

At the same time a Hindu dynasty was reigning in the northern part of Middle Java. The two regimes of different religions co-existed peacefully and were even united by marriage. The Hindu dynasty, the Sanjaya, built a Hindu equivalent of Boro-budur at Prambanan, about ten miles from Jogjakarta.

However, the quite predominant religion in Java, as every-where else in Indonesia except Bali, is that of Islam. We have exchanged the temple for the mosque, and the jaunty Balinese headgear of patterned batik, the *udeng*, for the sober black ovoid of the Moslem's brimless hat, the *pitji*.

The religion that Mohammed began in the Middle East in the seventh century spread to these Indies in the thirteenth century and the first Moslem kingdom arose in Java in the sixteenth.

Islam had reached India a century or so earlier, and it was in a somewhat Indianized form that it went on to these Indies. Here the Moslem faith, like Hinduism and Buddhism before it, underwent mutations that made it accord with the tolerant nature of a people averse to bigotry. One Indonesian scholar went so far as to write in 1963 that, in view of this attitude of tolerance, "It would not be surprising if there would be another religion in Indonesia teaching that Christ was a cousin of Lord Buddha or Siwa [Shiva]."[13]

Islam forbids the making of any pictures or statues of humans in a religious connection, so the stricter Moslems said that the shadow puppet play, the *wayang kulit*, must be prohibited. But this most popular of Indonesian village entertainments went on as before—with the puppeteers introducing some new stories with characters who were heroes from Islamic literature. At this time were introduced, also, wooden puppets, *wayang golek*.

JOGJAKARTA was only fifty minutes flight from Bali on the plane that went on to the much bigger capital city of Indonesia, Djakarta.

Jogja, as it is called, was the capital when the new republic was coming painfully to birth in the four years before 1950. It remains the cultural capital. Tourists for whom seeing Java was no more than an addendum to their Bali vacation usually found it more rewarding to spend their couple of days in the region of Jogjakarta rather than Djakarta.

The big hotel in Jogja was the Amburrukmo Palace. It had all the trimmings, from air conditioning to marble foyer and swimming-pool; but what it did not have, in my experience, was good service.

Golden Bali Tours had an office in the hotel and the amiable local manager, Mr Poerwoko, took me personally to one of the batik-making places—which are said to number nearly six hundred in and around Jogja. The one I went to, owned by a Mr Winotosastro, is extensive and well-run; many tourists are taken there and most make purchases in the showroom. It aids understanding of the waxing and dyeing process to be given a card with eight snippets of cloth affixed, the first a piece of white cambric and the eighth the finished batik print in a traditional brown-blue-beige pattern.

First the design is drawn. Then it is fashioned into a die made of copper strip. This is like an outsize flatiron about nine inches by seven, with a handle. A man stamps onto the cloth, in hot beeswax, the parts of the design that are to become brown. The yards-long piece is wax-printed all over in this way; and, at each stamping, the oblong "iron" must be placed down in precisely the right place so the pattern segments join exactly. All waxing of the cloth has to be done on both sides.

When the cloth goes to a girl who has a "pen" that flows hot wax, she waxes, in a different-coloured wax, the parts that will remain beige. Then the cloth is dyed and the unwaxed parts come out blue. All the first wax is scraped off the parts that will be brown. The parts that are to remain blue are waxed. Then the cloth goes into brown dye. The result looks awful—until the remaining wax is removed with boiling water and the intricate pattern becomes crisp and clear. Thus is a length, a single piece—not a roll or a bolt—of Javanese batik made, laboriously, tediously, and messily as to the wax scraping. Truly is it *hand*-made.

However, there are degrees of hand-making. With *batik*

69

tulis (meaning hand-drawn or hand-painted) even the first waxing is done by hand, the stamp not being used at all. *Tulis* is the most expensive kind.

This is the real thing in handcrafted batik and, considering the work that goes into it as well as the artistry of some of the designs (particularly the old ones), it should cost much more than it does. Some batik is created with *tjap* die-irons stamping the wax for each process, the cloth never going through the hands of the wax girls. The pattern is reproduced in a way that is, relatively, mechanical. Every section is exactly the same, whereas the wax pen, however meticulously it is used, will show the small variations that mark it as the handwork of an individual.

When, two days later, I went to Solo (Surakarta, but it is better known as Solo, 40 miles east of Jogja), there was the greatest variety of batiks on the stacked shelves of shop after shop. You could buy lengths of the stamped kind for less than a dollar.

In Jogja a man named Sutomo, who is physically very big for an Indonesian, has shortened his name to make his business Tom's Silverware, and more tourists would go to this silver factory than to any other. "Tom" Sutomo told me he had thirty-eight silversmiths. He paid them at daily rates ranging from 100 rupiahs (says, 20 cents or under 10 British pence) for learners who simply beat small billets of silver into flat ovals for bowl-making, to 900 rupiahs (say, $2 or £1) for the most highly skilled makers of bowls and bracelets and fashioners of rings. The silver, he said, was 85 per cent. He priced the wares according to weight and quality of workmanship. The most popular buys with tourists were bracelets.

ON THE WAY to Solo, we stop, only a short distance off the main road, at the great Hindu temples complex beside the village of Prambanan. These *chandi*, as ancient monuments are called, used to be spoken of as tenth-century but now there is evidence that they were built near the end of the ninth century. So they can be regarded as over a thousand years old.

There were originally eight major temples and a number of minor ones. The largest is a temple of Shiva, flanked by temples of the other two gods of the Hindu trinity, Brahma and Vishnu.

70

Shiva's temple rises as a great sculptured pinnacle to 157 feet. In these temples some, though by no means all, of the statues remain, the main ones being of the three gods, Shiva, Vishnu and four-headed and four-armed Brahma. Then there are some thirty panels of relief sculpture telling the *Ramayana* story.

These are on the balustrades of the Shiva and Brahma temples and many are in an excellent state of preservation. The panels of stone have been carved with great spirit and skill to portray the drama of the Hindu epic in a way that is expressively realistic and at the same time highly decorative, with stylized trees and richness of ornament.

So Prambanan is the perfect place to see the *Ramayana* danced as ballet. Nowhere else in Indonesia, Bali included, is the presentation as impressive as it is on the huge open-air stone stage that has the Shiva temple rising as on a backcloth and at a sufficient distance for all of it to be seen and without its being too distracting.

To see this *Ramayana* you must be there at full-moon time in the June-October months, when the four-part presentation runs for four nights, a different episode each night. I went with a guide from Golden Bali Tours and saw Episode III. It lasted from seven o'clock until nine.

The cast can be as many as six hundred and in Episode III a lot of the dancers are masked as monkey warriors of the white monkey general, Hanuman. Giants and "fairies" come prominently into the story; there is more than one large corps of beautiful maidens many of whom are, indeed, beautiful. And a great many snakes and eagles appear. The costuming was brilliant and Prince Rama a most handsome and shiningly-accoutred hero, with magic bow. Being an incarnation of Vishnu, Rama can shoot an arrow into the ocean and dry up the sea between his kingdom and the one where his beloved Sita is being held prisoner by the wicked king of the giants, Rahwono. There are battles between giants and monkeys—the balletic fights are excellent and some brilliant clowning is part of them—and between eagles and snakes. The hero of this episode is really the wicked Rahwono's giant brother Kumbokarno, who is a match for a thousand monkeys. He has to be magic-arrowed in the end by Rama's brother, Leksmana, but both respect his valour and pray for his soul as it ascends to heaven on the song of a great chorus of fairy-maidens scattering sweet-smelling flowers.

To the extent that there is some vocalization and not all movements are choreographic, the performance was not strictly, or not entirely, ballet; but it could not be called opera. The spot- and flood-lighting was good, and the gamelan music most effective.

However, the seats are stone. To be comfortably seated for two hours you need a cushion—perhaps a blow-up air ring would do—or a naturally well-padded posterior, which I lack, and I found the seat achingly hard. Cushions should either be provided or a concessionaire allowed to hire them out to patrons. You also need a story-programme (such as I had from GBT) and a pocket torch to read it by, or a guide to tell you what is happening. Some American tourists sitting in front of us said they were quite at a loss as they had no idea of the *Ramayana* story.

Prambanan's complex is the biggest Hindu temple construc- tion in Indonesia (not that it would look outstandingly big in India). Although the principal form of ornament is like a bell with a handle that is clearly the stone *lingam* of Hinduism, there are Buddhist touches to the architecture and, in fact, a Buddhist temple complex on a smaller scale was erected close by what are called the Chandi Lara (or Loro or Roro) Djonggrang temples. As one scholar wrote, "It seemed that two religions lived and developed peacefully side by side."[5]

For centuries the Shiva temple at Prambanan was in ruins, possibly as a result of a big earthquake that is said to have oc- curred in 1584. Restoration begun in 1918 in an exploratory fashion was completed in 1953. Restoration of other temples is still going on.

THE ROAD TO SOLO (Surakarta) had ox-carts with rattan sides and a wide roof on top and wooden yokes for the white zebu cattle that pulled them, the same humped beasts that pull ploughs through the mud of the ricefields and look too cleanly and fine-boned for the work that the wallowing water-buffalo with its coarse dun hide looks right for.

72

Flanking the road are fields of rice—rice of special quality, very white, and the Javanese say, "Klaten rice has the best smell." As well as rice there are fields of tobacco, sugarcane, corn, cassava, soya beans, coffee, cotton, peanuts, melons, fruit-trees: I even saw a few sheep. This is some of the most fertile land in Java—which means, such is the fertility of Java, some of the most fertile in the world.

My GBT guide's name is Chamdi, pronounced Hamdi. Has he a forename I can call him by? He smiles and says no. (Sukarno had only one name and so has the president now, Suharto.) But, Chamdi says, I can call him *Mas*. This is like an Australian suggesting you should call him "Mate"; and, it being a term of such familiarity, you don't use it unless you are invited to. Incidentally, only villagers and children call you *Tuan*, or your wife *Njonja* (with *j* pronounced as *y*) or your daughter *Nona* for "Miss". The English-speakers use "Mister", which is the best usage for us when addressing, say, an Indonesian business-man.

"You see that bird, there in the cage," the guide says as the car stops behind an ox-cart for another one to pass, and I look up at what is like a small pigeon. "We call it *perkutut*. We Javanese love this bird for bringing good luck and for its singing. Except it is unlucky if it sings at night. There is a competition through all Indonesia for the best singing *perkutut*. To buy a good one in the market costs a thousand rupiahs. But the prize for the best singer in Indonesia is two hundred thousand rupiahs, about five hundred dollars American."

The city known as Solo is officially Surakarta, which is not such a good name but avoids confusion with the Solo River, which the city is on. It is the longest river in Java. Surakarta was the capital until, in the eighteenth century, the local Sultan quarrelled with his uncle who built Jogjakarta; but it remains a heart-place of Javanese culture. It is also, Mas Chamdi said, famous for its pretty girls. "We have a song that says, 'The girls from Solo walk like a hungry tiger'. Slow and sexy."

We went first to the Kraton of the Pangeran, which means Palace of the Prince. Called the Kraton Mangku Negara, this place is extensive but hardly palatial. Visitors could be admitted, if they asked, to where the prince's "antiques" were in glass cases; but the lights were not switched on. And one does not go to Java to see Murano glass.

We had left there and the car was honking its way past three men moving a log of wood as big as a telegraph pole on a small handcart, one sweating between the shafts and the other two with their torsoes wet from pushing. I asked about the Sultan.

In Solo the Sultan is called the Susuhunan. His Highness's name, which means "Nail of the World", is Paku Buwono XII, the twelfth of his line.

Solo dancing is said to be very good and distinctive Court dances are sometimes held at this *kraton*, which has a famous gamelan orchestra. The adjoining Royal Museum had some fascinating exhibits, few of which were adequately labelled or lit. I particularly liked the wedding craft in which some *susuhunans* made nuptial voyages. Its prow was a face with an enormous black moustache.

A much better *kraton*, though, was the one I saw back at Jogja, whose Sultan, His Highness Hamengku Buwono IX, was the Minister of Economy, Finance and Industry. Here the roof of the marble-floored reception pavilion is rayed like the sun and very handsome. Moreover, the *kraton* has what is reputedly the finest antique gamelan in Java. But it plays only one week a year; and there is another one that plays only at wedding ceremonies of the Sultan's children. The first Sultan's palanquins, in which he used to be carried to the mosque, are so rococo in vermilion and gold that they are absurdly beautiful.

There is also a lovely little State coach, of European make, ornamented with the bust of a young lady, and known by a name that translates as Honourable Fair Lady Fetish. Fresh flower offerings are placed before it daily, and in March each year the coach is ceremonially washed. This is done in public, and people collect the washing water in tins and bottles and sprinkle it over themselves. Believing that the water gains elixir properties from the wooden fair lady on the royal vehicle, some even drink a little of it.

Some architectural curiosa do not quite make the place a Javanese Brighton, but the exotica range from a rotunda, which Good Queen Victoria might have thought pretty, to the iron-work shelter for the grotesque and undeniably Hindu giant

74

who stands guard, clad in Silvafros, in a Moslem court.

What I think Solo has ahead of Jogja is even-brighter *betjaks*. These are the pedicabs, such as an Irishman might be tempted to define as a bicycle with three wheels, two of them on its sidecar which is in front. There is a hood over the two-passenger seat and the rear wheel has a large mudguard or fender there is no real functional need for. But this will have painted on it in the gaudiest colours a tropical scene, perhaps, and the *betjak*'s name. It was in names that Solo had the edge. I felt sure that I had seen among the pedicabs of Jogjakarta a ROCKET, a NEW LOOK, an ATOMIC and I had little doubt that Jogja could also produce a CAPITOL, a GREYHOUND, and perhaps even a KING KONG. But I couldn't imagine that anywhere else but Solo was there a *betjak* called SSH, or one with the semantically eccentric name of NORMAL.

Solo's main shopping centre was entered through an engaging white arch with the Sultan's initials and crest on it, and the city had a likeable air. As mentioned earlier, it is a great place to buy batiks cheaply.

One is inclined to expect more of Islamic architecture than it has in Indonesia: Malaysia is much better in this respect. In Java, Solo's mosque is the only one with a minaret.

FOR THE DIENG PLATEAU it was an early start, six o'clock on a Sunday morning. Not that Sunday made any difference, because the Moslem sabbath is on Friday. The road out of Jogja was busy with *betjaks* and just bicycles, the two- and four-wheel carts called *dokars* and *andongs,* and vendors jog-jogging with such shoulder-pole burdens as the great tin canisters that hold the *krupuk* mixture the housewife fries into the airy "bread" of the Indies.

"The best *krupuk* comes from near Surabaja in East Java," said Mas Chamdi, who was again my guide, on a GBT tour that took a full day, covered about 170 miles and cost $50 whether you were one person or four like the family in the other car ahead. Our car was a Chevrolet Impala with American left-hand drive, which is right for right-side-of-the-road driving; but in Java they drive on the left, and fast, around 100 kilometres (62 miles) an hour, with the horn going most of the time

75

in built-up areas and skittering chickens missing death by centi-metres. But all the tour-car drivers I had drove very well.

This is one of the most populous regions of the most populous island of Indonesia. The fields of growing foodstuffs seem to look askance at the ground taken up by cemeteries—Moslem, Chinese, and much-smaller Christian. In Java, unlike Bali, there is no cremation. And no cockfighting. And no bare breasts, even of the old women. Nor any functioning Hindu temples; only the mosques that seem so infrequent because some are hardly noticeable, because they are no higher than houses, and not all have an onion dome to support Islam's symbol of the sickle moon and star.

Out of town near the Krasak River a sign says WELCOME TO CENTRAL JAVA. The river is bouldered with lava thrown out in the 1969 eruption of the volcano that looms on our right. Merapi is 9,500 feet, and one of the thirty-five places of volcanic activity in Java. But serious eruptions have not been many.

The town of Magelang has traffic lights. A man waits for the green and then crosses the street carrying on his back a brand-new wooden bed. A calico banner announces AUTO RALLY at, of all places, Borobudur, the great Buddhist monument we'll see on the way back from the plateau we're going to, up from the plain to 6,500 feet.

We stop beyond Wonosobo, at 2,500 feet, for coffee. The rest-house garden looks down on just about the last of the rice terraces, coconuts and banana palms. We are already high enough for tea-growing. And bicycles have disappeared: it is too hilly.

It is cooler again, crisp after the humidity of the plain, when there is another stop higher up. From a viewing place you look down a precipice of air onto the black roofs—corrugated iron painted black—of a big village at the foot of the steepest moun-tainside. Steep though it is, the mountainside is gardened, terraced, a stairway of cultivation, mainly vegetables and white-flowering pyrethrum, chrysanthemum's cousin that produces the base for insecticide. And the sky opens to show Gunung Sumbing's ten-thousand-foot head that is soon closed over again with clouds.

The palms have given way to acacias and casuarinas. Farmers

76

These ruins of Hindu temples on the Dieng Plateau are twelve hundred years old and are believed to have been Java's first stone buildings.
CENTRAL JAVA   Author's Ektachromes
Sulphurous steam rises from a muddy pool of boiling water in the highlands of Java, which still has a number of active volcanoes.

Statue of Vishnu at the ninth-century Hindu temple complex of Prambanan, outside Jogjakarta.

CENTRAL JAVA

Borobudur has about 1,400 sculptured scenes from the life of Buddha. This shows his mother, Queen Maya.

Borobudur, the
What looks like

Prambanan's carved stone
legend, the Ramayana.

dous monument of Buddhistic art, was raised about twelve hundred years ago.
ural mountainside is full of cave-like niches containing statues of the seated Buddha.

Author's Ektachromes

lustrate the greatest Hindu   Bell-like stone dagobs on top of Borobudur are silhouetted
rving is rich and vital.   at evening against a horizon of Java's mountains.

Roofed carts, drawn by the humped Brahman breed of cattle, were passed along the road between Jogjakarta and Solo (Surakarta).
CENTRAL JAVA   Author's Ektachromes
Batik maker at Jogjakarta waxing a design. Her "pen" flows hot wax onto every line of the pattern, retained when the cloth is dyed.

in conical hats, men and women, work hillside plots of corn. Tobacco dries on wooden racks by the roadside. Cabbages pile out of baskets on women's backs. The people's skins look darker and their faces less bland than those of the Javanese down on the plain.

The road climbs and climbs, then flattens out and we come to Dieng.

UP HERE on the roof of Central Java some twelve hundred years ago men were sculpturing the statues of Hindu gods and setting them on small temples. The architects and stone carvers must have come from India. Not only is the style of the structures utterly Indian, but the Javanese had never made stone buildings. These on the Dieng Plateau were the first. Perhaps some were erected in the seventh century; but the guide said the ones we came to, the principal ones, were eighth century.

Four of these shrines—they seemed rather small to be "temples"—stood isolated on a tiny plain of their own in a saucer of hills near the village of Dieng. They stood up blackly against the light and the pale grass, four ruins in a row, not very high, rather squat. There were stone foundations of other buildings that were quite gone, and perhaps were where priests lived or pilgrims stayed. Dieng was a place of pilgrimage: there was never a city up here.

At close quarters the dark stone, hoary with lichens, shows ornate pilasters and niches that held statues, now taken away. The only figure I can find is a rather fine relief of Shiva. A number of statues and carvings are gathered into a nearby pavilion: they stand on the ground or on shelves, without any identification. The elephant-headed Ganesh is here, and the ubiquitous *lingam* columns. Under one of these that was slotted into a stone *yoni* the archaeologists found human ashes which they thought were the remains of a king.

Beyond the ruins there was what looked at first glance like a settlement of new houses. But they were made of woven palm-leaf, sides and roof, all of matting on a wooden frame, and with no windows or chimneys and only a door at the end. There were dozens of them, and more being made, for a new Dieng industry —mushroom-growing.

We went on to see hot springs. The eyes of the two children in the other car with their Australian parents, John and Mary Walters of Perth, widened at the furious cauldron of mud-grey water that boiled and bubbled and leapt and whorled and threw off a cloud of smoke that smelt pungently of sulphur.

Lunch was a picnic, with food the hotel had put up in boxes, at a quiet place in a reserve formed by a horseshoe lake that shone bright blue in the sunlight. In one part the water was warm, from subterranean activity coming through.

Then we descended from this high, cool calm. Down between the mountainsides terraced with broad beans and corn, back to the plains of cocopalms, perspiration, bicycles and emerald tables of riceland.

Turning off at Magelang brought us to the great sculptural man-made mount called Borobudur.

YOUNG NATIONS—and, apart from the war-torn Vietnam republics, Indonesia is the youngest nation in Asia—are always fervently nationalistic and full of patriotic pride in what their country is and has. This, while it is understandable enough and worthy, can lead to blowing big notes of hyperbole when they trumpet forth their tourist attractions.

Take Borobudur. According to the booklet[16] one buys there (and it has the blessing of the Indonesian Archaeological Service) Borobudur is the "equal of Angkor Wat and Bayon", those masterpieces of Khmer architecture in Cambodia. "The grandeur of Borobudur is beyond description," says the writer, and it is "undoubtedly the finest and most significant monument in the Southern Hemisphere".

Admittedly, just about every great construction one can think of is in the Northern Hemisphere. But surely Peru's ruins of Machu Picchu, the "lost [until 1912] city of the Incas" could be regarded as more significant. Further, some of the tourist literature claims that Borobudur is "the largest Buddhist temple in the world".[7] Angkor Wat is larger and, although it was built as a Hindu temple, it was converted into a Buddhist one in the twelfth century.

However, Borobudur "is described as the most magnificent monument of Buddhistic art in the whole of Asia," says the

78

Encyclopaedia Britannica,[18] and as having "terraces and galleries sculptured with a wonderful series of bas-reliefs". "This work must have occupied hundreds of artists over a period of several generations. It depicts scenes from the life of Buddha and the legends of his reincarnation—more than 200 panels in all. . . . The straightforward artistry of these reliefs may be compared to the best in Gothic art."

Indian sculpture, which this is (not Indonesian), had been ahead of sculpture in western (not eastern) Europe for at least two thousand years. Europe was in the Dark Ages when Borobudur's reliefs were carved, around the year 800.

The meaning of the name Borobudur is vague: the *boro* part is thought to mean "a complex of temples or monasteries or dormitories" and *budur* indicates "high" or "on a hill". Actually, it *is* a hill, a hill of architectural and sculptural stone, glorifying the Buddha and his life of virtue through renunciation of fleshly desire. (Buddhism, with its monastic passiveness, seems to have come about as a reaction from the sensuality, violence and sacrificial bloodiness of Hinduism.)

Borobudur was probably built, at the end of the eighth century, by kings of the Sailendra dynasty, who were Mahayana Buddhists. The hill, some experts say, was man-raised, not natural. It was terraced and clad with stone in the form of a low stepped pyramid, with sides about four hundred feet long at the base. It rises in receding tiers for six straight storeys. Then there are three more levels that are concentric rings of *dagobs*, each like a great stone bell with a handle. These are big enough to each contain a larger-than-lifesize statue of the seated Buddha, and there are 72 of them, and they are latticed with holes, some square, some diamond-shaped. Topping the structure is an outsize *dagob* or *stupa* about thirty feet in diameter and over twenty feet high. To its pinnacle the overall height above ground is about 135 feet.

When you look up at Borobudur you do not get any impression of a pyramid, for the top of the crowning stupa barely protrudes above what looks rather like a sculptural mountainside full of caves. These are niches and each contains, or did contain, a seated-Buddha statue. There is something almost phantasmagoric about this repetition of forms, as though one suddenly had multiple vision.

In the middle of each side is a stairway. You should not go straight up but turn off at each tier. Relief sculptures are all along the walls and the balustrades, in panels. Superbly carved here, in more than a hundred panels, is the life of the Buddha, and many other panels portray the lives of several Bodhisattvas (Buddhas-to-be). A listing of what is depicted in no less than 120 of these panels was to be found in the back of the small booklet that was on sale called *Glimpses of the Borobudur* by Soediman.[15] But it would be unwise to spend all one's time with these reliefs and not go to the top of the monument. The view I saw to the north was magnificent, with the very high range of Central Java's mountains in dark blue silhouette.

The little book says there are eleven series of reliefs consisting of not less than 1,460 scenes—perhaps rather much of a good thing. Prambanan's relief sculptures are more deeply carved, more active: Borobudur's Buddhistic art is quieter, with the figures less individualized, tending to be stereotypes. In a panel described as "The daughters of Mara attempt to seduce the Bodhisattva with lustful dances", the girls, one feels, would have been much more seductive had they been carved for a Hindu temple. But these panels are often beautifully composed, and the attendant embellishment is better than in the Prambanan panels. At times the motifs' richness suggests embroidery in stone.

With a shock of concern I read, "Borobudur is in great danger! Borobudur must be saved!" This was exclaimed by the Director of the Archaeological Service of Indonesia, Drs R. Soekmono[15] who said, "A total restoration is strictly necessary." What is feared, apparently, is that water's gradual erosion of the piled earth underneath will cause the stone to slide off the man-made hill. If that happened Borodbudur would "go into oblivion"—again. So unconcerned with it last century were the Moslem Javanese that it was a half-buried ruin when Sir Stamford Raffles became interested in Borobudur during his five-year rule of the Java the French had taken from the Dutch, to whom the British returned it; and it was the Dutch who restored Borobudur.

Assuming that Borobudur's peril is as stated, one would

fervently hope that the estimated cost of this restoration work, $5½ million, is contributed.

One feels about such places as Borobudur, the Pyramids in Egypt and Angkor Wat—where the Khmer kings are said to have made wars in order to capture enough prisoners to be slaves to build those temples—that it would be appalling if anything raised with such an immensity of labour and amplitude of art was allowed to fall down into a stoneheap.

Passing through Djakarta

A QUESTION posed by air connections was: Should I spend only a night in Djakarta or stay there for several days?

Nothing I had read about Indonesia's capital city suggested that it was worth a stay of several days. The most reliable guidebook said that the tropical fish market "provides one of the most attractive spectacles in a city that otherwise does not offer much to sightseers". It went on to say: "Under President Sukarno's regime New Djakarta was lavishly endowed with monuments built regardless of cost and uniformly appalling."

However, the *Golden Guide*[17] thought highly of the Hotel Indonesia, calling it, ". . . one of the Sukarno regime's supreme achievements. The various halls have been splendidly decorated by Indonesian painters and sculptors: notice at the left of the entrance the remarkably beautiful mural depicting life in Bali."

I stayed at the Indonesia, another Inter-Continental operation, and can confirm that it was impressively decorated. Moreover, it had the reputation of being particularly well managed by a most experienced hotelier, Desmond Coleman.

Big as the Indonesia was (400+ rooms), two bigger hotels were building in Djakarta: the Banteng (the name of a wild ox found in Java and Borneo) and the Hotel Duta Merlin which would have over 1,000 rooms and was expected to open for the PATA* Conference to be held in Djakarta in 1974.

* Pacific Area Travel Association.

On the way from the airport, where a forty-minute Garuda flight from Jogjakarta had landed me, Djakarta looked specially big, bustling and chaotic after the smaller city and Bali. That it had a population of five million people seemed all too believable. Every bus was packed. The *betjaks* were grey-painted and had numbers on them: they were not, as the Jogja-Solo betjaks were, picturesque. In other areas of Djakarta, the *betjaks* are red, blue, green, yellow or white. Only *betjaks* of the area colour can ply for hire within that area. This is to minimize traffic congestion.

Moslem sultans in 1527 called a trading town near the mouth of a West Java river Djaya-Karta meaning "Place of Victory", and in 1602 lost it to the Dutch, who rechristened it Batavia. I had spent one night there in 1948 on the way back from an assignment in north Borneo and remembered it mainly for its dirty brown canals, and Dutchmen drinking Bols in wicker chairs in the old Hôtel des Indes.

The capital I was driven round at night in a Nitour car was a vastly larger city. The canals were still whiffy, but decorative with reflections of neon signs. These perch on the high-rise buildings that march down the Djalan Thamrin, the main drag, and spangle the night scene with all the gaudy colours of a Western modern metropolis. To Indonesians it is a city crammed with such exciting exotica as drive-in movies, bowling alleys, 24-hour coffee bars, horse racing, greyhound racing, jai-alai and golf courses, as well as night clubs with strip tease (which was not permitted in Jogjakarta) and gambling casinos.

The Western visitor, spurning such home-grown diversions, can find in Djakarta the Javanese opera and Ramayana ballet, the shadow-show *wayang kulit* and also the *wayang golek*, the wooden-puppet show; and the distinctive Sundanese dancing of West Java. An initial impression that Djakarta was culturally deprived did not survive my night visit to the Cultural Centre, where there are not only theatres and concert halls but an exhibition of Australian books.

From there I was picked up by the Nitour car with a bright-minded, English-fluent guide whose first name was Harry and who said, "We had better show you the Bina Ria area." Bina means to develop or promote, Ria is gaiety or joy.

82

This seemed to be on the edge of town and consisted of night-clubs, bars, tents and girls standing round in mini-skirts, puffing cigarettes and fluttering false eyelashes and, some of them, still not managing to look older than sixteen, which Harry said some of them weren't. The less glamorous ones could be had for as little as 500 rupiahs, which is scarcely more than a dollar. You went in a tent hire of which cost Rp.250. Picking up a hostess at a plushy nightclub and going to a motel could cost 10,000 rupes, over twenty dollars.

The tents of Bina Ria have now been removed, as a result of agitation against prostitution by women's organizations. The prostitutes remain, but have to be taken to motels or hotels, outside the area.

From Tokyo to Djakarta, which is catching up fast, the place where West (male) meets East (female) is, increasingly, the steambath/massage parlour. (A steambath is only a steambath but a massage can be, but is not necessarily, more than a massage.) These places have proliferated in Djakarta and, significantly, a number are near the big hotels. They have such names as Venus, Paradise, Aloha, Bangkok, Ginza, Florida—there was even one with an Indonesian name, Dusit Thani. Rates were about $7 an hour; and apparently there were enough customers who considered the services were worth that.

There is a considerable Chinatown that I saw only the fringe of. As well as Chinese eating-places, Djakarta has more places than anywhere else in Indonesia for eating Indonesian food.

What I do regret not seeing in Djakarta is the national Museum. This, I am told, is very good indeed and worth several hours of inspection—which needs to be in the morning, because it closes, surprisingly, at one o'clock (and on Mondays does not open at all).

What you can't miss seeing in Djakarta—it stands 384 feet high in Merdeka (Freedom) Square—is the national monument. It is topped with a gold symbol of a flame, covered with 70 pounds weight of 22-carat gold in the form of gold leaf.

There is more to Djakarta than I have mentioned, says my friend Lie of the Golden Bali Tours, whose head office is in the Hotel Indonesia, and whose executive director is a remarkable woman, Mrs Hanny Malkan. Lie thinks that Djakarta has been singularly lucky in its Governor Ali Sadikin, who has done much to improve the city.

GAMBLING CASINOS in Djakarta are supposed to be for foreigners only. Officially, Indonesians are not allowed to frequent them, though rich ones do. The casino operations are aimed at extracting money from such foreigners as Singaporean and Malaysian Chinese, who are notably fond of casino gambling.

Any other foreigners who, being in Singapore, wished to gamble in Djakarta, could participate in a scheme that in mid-1972 was giving them every encouragement to do so. You had only to buy a thousand Singapore dollars (around $300 Aust.) worth of chips from a selling agent of the casino operators, N.I.A.C. (New International Amusement Centre) and you would be given an air ticket Singapore-Djakarta return, free accommodation with breakfast at a medium-class Djakarta hotel, free transport to any of the N.I.A.C. casinos, where drinks and snacks would also be provided "on the house".

Stakes were high: Rp. 2,000 or $US 5 was the minimum bet at the least of the blackjack tables.

THOSE WHO TOUR from Djakarta usually go about forty miles south to Bogor, where the botanic gardens laid out in 1827 beside a palace the Dutch built are spread over 275 acres and grow 10,000 species of plants and trees. Bogor is a lush, heavy rainfall area, and the orchid house has several thousand varieties. The Perth couple I had met on the Dieng tour from Jogja, John and Mary Waters, went there and kindly sent me a report. Bogor's gardens were "really very beautiful". The rest of their tour took them to the Puntjak mountain area and this they found enjoyable; but they thought the trip to the Dieng Plateau was more so.

North Sumatra

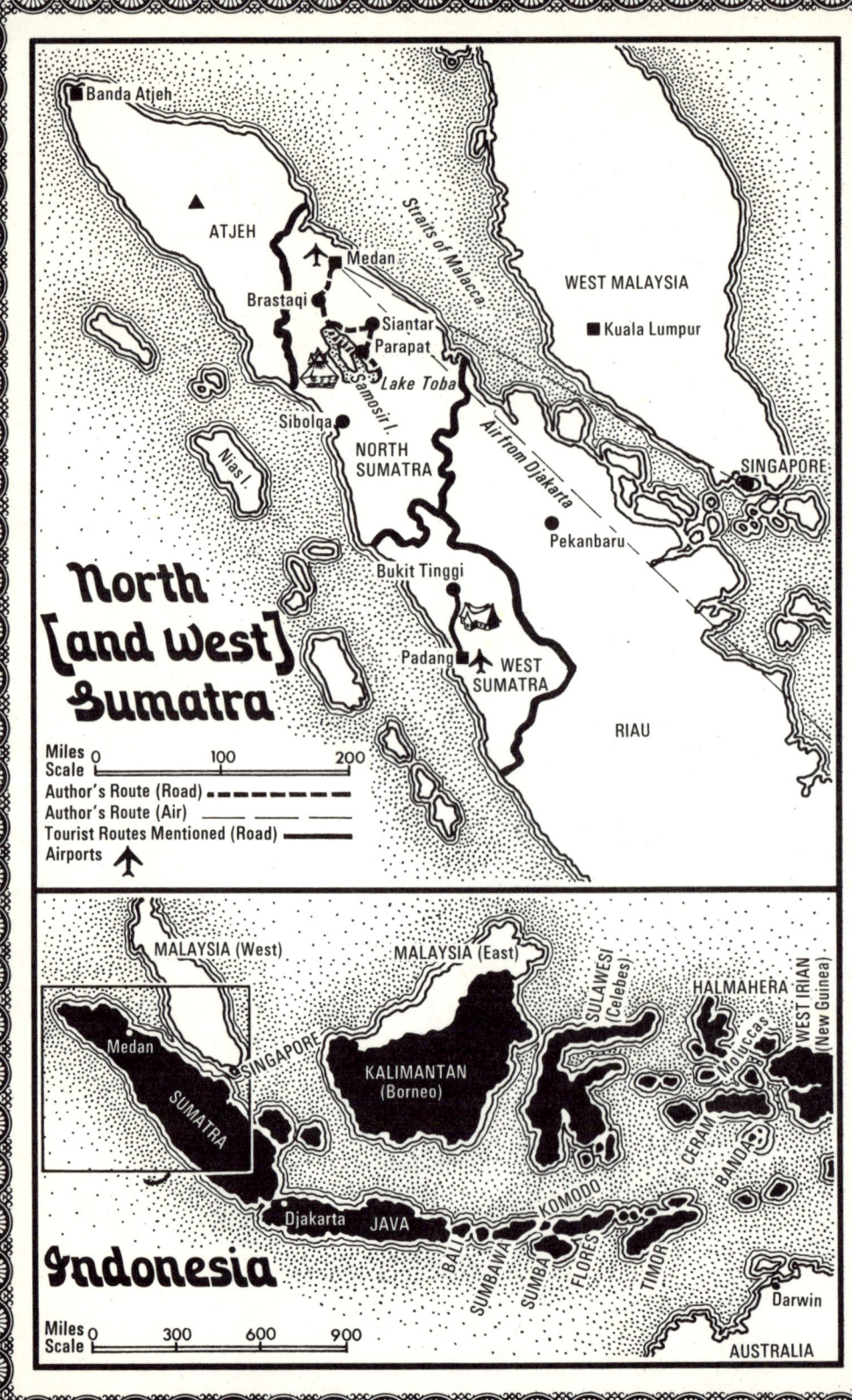

North [and west] Sumatra

Banda Atjeh

ATJEH

Medan

Brastaqi

Siantar
Parapat

Samosir I.

Lake Toba

Sibolqa

NORTH
SUMATRA

Nias I.

Bukit Tinggi

Padang

WEST
SUMATRA

RIAU

Straits of Malacca

WEST MALAYSIA

Kuala Lumpur

Air from Djakarta

SINGAPORE

Pekanbaru

Miles
Scale   0   100   200

Author's Route (Road) ------
Author's Route (Air)
Tourist Routes Mentioned (Road) ——
Airports

Indonesia

MALAYSIA (West)

MALAYSIA (East)

SULAWESI
(Celebes)

HALMAHERA

WEST IRIAN
(New Guinea)

Medan

SINGAPORE

KALIMANTAN
(Borneo)

Moluccas

SUMATRA

CERAM

BANDA

Djakarta   JAVA

BALI

SUMBAWA

SUMBA

KOMODO

FLORES

TIMOR

Darwin

AUSTRALIA

Miles
Scale   0   300   600   900

Horned houses by Lake Toba

FOUR-THIRTY A.M. The car has slid through the quiet dark of a sleeping Djakarta to an airport lounge packed with people and crackling with voices. You should have been here half an hour earlier, but could not believe that you were required to check in an hour before take-off for a domestic flight. Yes, you are told, one hour before: the planes are full. See that queue . . . those are people who've come out on the chance of getting a cancellation or a latecomer's seat.

You wonder why so many people want to fly to Sumatra at five o'clock in the morning. As you go aboard the Garuda DC-9, and as the roaring cocoon full of people soars up into the dawnlight, you are still a bit surprised that you are flying there yourself. Sumatra may have the tourist potential you've been told it has, but it is hardly on the tourist track yet.

Sumatra is Ultima Thule in these Indies. North Sumatra, where you're going, is the western extremity of the Indonesian archipelago. It is big, though, Sumatra: not an island like Bali that you might have difficulty finding on the map. From the eastern end you are over very soon after leaving Djakarta, to Medan where you are going, is about a thousand miles. Sumatra is almost the size of Spain. It would make three and a half Javas—and has only a quarter of Java's population. Much of Sumatra is jungled mountains, which run the length on the Indian Ocean (pardon, Indonesian Ocean since Sukarno) side of this long island that might be said to look on the map like a stumpy-tailed, pregnant crocodile.

Sumatra is beginning to move out of the Maugham-type novel, the oil-industry handbook, the rubber- and timber-getters' gazetteer and into the tourist guide-book. As yet in the *Golden Guide to South & East Asia* Sumatra gets only one page out of 500 pages. Its main tourist attractions are Lake Toba and the Batak people's remarkable houses in North Sumatra.

This plane appears to have only two other European passengers. They don't look like tourists. They are white-shirt types who could be Goodyear Rubber accountants going out to do an audit at the Deli plantation. Next to me is the most aromatic Indian lady. The flowers she carries are tropically fragrant, and she laves her arms with a heavily sweet-scented pomade. Tobacco fumes and the faint smell of the proffered airline coffee fight back unavailingly. Night reddens into day and overcast obscures the geography of Sumatra until we come down through grey nothingness of cloud to the sight of a tapeworm river eating its way through sodden, palm-studded green that now has the geometry of the airport of Medan (pronounced Maydan).

I AM MET by a representative of Nitour, which is Indonesia's "official" tourist organization, the big one, and the one that could be (but isn't) the Indonesian equivalent of Cooks.

I want to change some money. I go, with a Nitour guide, to the Bank of Indonesia. I have Australian-dollars Travellers Cheques and sterling Travellers Cheques (Cooks, both) and I have Australian notes and Bank of England notes—no U.S. currency because it is in process of being devalued, and I do not regard it as a good bet. But the Bank of Indonesia in Medan will not change anything but American dollars. They don't want Australian money or sterling in any form; they do not even know the exchange rates of these currencies. So I am taken to a money changer, a handsome Indian who is also an airline representative. He offers me 425 rupiahs to the Aust. dollar I have been exchanging in Bali for 460, and the rate is going up.*

* In September 1972 the rate was *officially* Rp. 495 to the Aust. dollar, but what you got was about 470. The American dollar was 415 rupiahs, and the pound sterling 1018.

I can't get the Indian higher than 440, and have to take that rate. The hotel I go to will cash only American-dollars Travellers Cheques. But, I find out later from two New Zealand business men staying at the hotel, who are pretty disgruntled about the whole business, that the Bank Dagang Negara (Commerical State Bank) will exchange rupiahs for Australian, N.Z. or sterling TCs or notes. But Nitour didn't know that.

MEDAN, the chief city of Sumatra, has nothing much to keep the tourist there. It gives the impression of not being big enough to hold a population of 900,000. More than a quarter of these are Chinese and about 50,000 are Indians.

By mid-morning I am on my way by car to Lake Toba, which is 147 miles (235 kilometres) by the road we'll take, and about 35 miles shorter by another road that will be the return route. I have with me a young Sumatran guide who speaks English. His mellifluous name is Rismono Trio. Taking only a small bag for a two-night stay, I have left my suitcase at the Hotel Dirga Surya, a name I ask Rismono the meaning of.

"It means 'Congratulations sunlight'," he says.

I hope Rismono's translation of Dirga Surya is correct, and think the name should be Anglicized. Travellers' tales would be less boring if one could start off with: "I remember, up in North Sumatra, meeting a very odd bod when I was staying in Medan at the Hotel Congratulations Sunlight. . . ."

As we run out of the city I try to read an information sheet on Medan I have been presented with, prepared by the North Sumatra Tourist Guide Association (Nosutoga). It turns out to be a short (but not short enough) account of the Sulthanate (not sultanate) of Deli, the province we are in. There is a legendary bit about a princess in a glass coffin but, historically, it becomes dull in the most meticulous way, e.g.: "On August 28th 1888 Sulthan Maamun Alrasjid founded the new Sulthan Deli's castle at Medan . . . and on May 18th 1891 transferred all governmental activities. . . ." Anyway, the sulthanate no longer exists since Indonesian independence. And the former Sulthan's Palace was in a very messy state of repair, not open to visitors, not worth visiting.

We are now beyond the shanty-town suburbs of Medan, the

cocopalms have thickened and we are no longer passing ox carts with turbaned Indian drivers, or houses with harsh roofs of corrugated iron. Now the houses are thatched with nipa-palm, and their walls are mainly bamboo. We are in the region called Karo.

The Karonese belong to the large tribal group of Batak people. Their country now has the smotheringly thick, lush vegetation we call jungle. It contains monkeys galore, the occasional orang-utan and the rare, rather small tiger. In terrain less overgrown, Sumatra also has the rhinoceros. This jungle doubtless contains the largest flower in the world, the *Rafflesia* that grows from a groundling vine a bloom eighteen inches across, and stinks to high heaven.

Twenty-five miles out of Medan we stop where, at Sibolangit, a jungle botanical garden has been created by the simple expedient of clearing a couple of paths into jungle that would otherwise be too thick to enter. Walking along these paths you can see how luxuriant is the growth, how thick are the liana vines that loop splendid trees like the buttressed *turi-turi* (the Sumatran oak), and how vivid is the betel palm's upper section, where the green trunk turns vermilion. This is truly tropical jungle, such as one sees in Borneo but not in Bali.

The road climbs out of the lowland ricefields that are ploughed with water-buffaloes here, not oxen. The people have much the same Malay-cast features you see in Java. But here the sarongs they wear are not batik-printed cotton but woven.

School is out at the village of Petjeren. Unused to tourists, the children stop their play to gather round me and gape. Point a camera and the little girls scamper off squealing. Boys stand their ground, a mixture of smiles and dourness. But there is something here more cameraworthy.

It is a house, the first Batak traditional *rumah bolon* (big house) I have seen. It looks as wide as it is long and high. What is so striking is its angular shape. The peaked gable projects forward, from a great roof of black thatch greened with moss. Beneath this, the wooden sidewalls slope down. The entrance is by ladder-like steps. Rismono says six families live in the house. It looks big enough to hold them.

To the west smoke rises from a towering mountain. About

a dozen Sumatran volcanoes remain active and Sibajak (nearly 7,500 feet) is one that is always smoking. Not far away is Sinabung, a higher mountain and also active. Volcanic effusion makes for fertility. Flowers are as flourishing as the corn and the cabbages in these Karo Highlands. The gardened grounds are attractive at the Dutch-built resthouse we come to at Bukit (Hill or Mountain) Kubu (Tent). No one is staying there and if we want lunch it will have to be brought in from the Chinese restaurant in the town, Brastagi. So, I figure, it will save time if we go into Brastagi and eat there, at the Chinese restaurant— which we do. It has that peculiar ugliness that Chinese restaurants contrive, usually with the aid of blue paint and calendars. Tea comes in a glass too hot to hold, with a saucer the tea is tipped into and drunk from that. However, three *nasi gorengs* (guide and driver join me) cost not much more than a dollar.

In the middle of Brastagi's main street is a long fruit stall built in the extended shape of a Batak *bolon* house and having at its frontal peak a water-buffalo's horned head. This is for tourists, the passing-through types bound for Lake Toba like myself, and the Sumatrans who come up to Brastagi as a resort place that, at 4,500 feet, is much cooler than Medan. There is also a very large pavilion-type hall in Batak style that is an imposing example of this distinctive architecture.

Back on the road, we often pass women coming from the fields. The hoes they use, with large square blades, they carry balanced on their heads. A woman may carry several hoes in this way, the blades resting on a skull-pad of towelling, the long handles sticking up behind. Seldom is there a man to be seen. I ask why.

"The Karo men," Rismono says, "they stay at home and drink and play chess."

"Chess?"

"Yes, they like very much to play chess. These people learn to play chess from the Portuguese in the olden days."

"What do they drink?"

"*Tuak*. It is a beer they make here from the sap of the sugar palm. You can buy a bottle for ten rupiahs." Less than three cents.

"What's their religion? Mostly Moslems?"

"In this region about seventy per cent of the Karonese are Christians".

We pass some Dutch-style wooden churches along the road. They look gawky and strange, and the landscape heathen with its flamboyant growth under bright blue skies that arch to horizons peaked with mountains such as the Netherlands never knew.

We leave the main road and go off ten kilometres to a dramatic viewing place. This gives a first sight of Lake Toba and, far down below, a village near its shores. What can be seen of the mountain-rimmed lake, nearly 3,000 feet above sea level, suggests a body of water like an inland sea. And, indeed, it is large—more than fifty miles long and nearly twenty miles wide. And it is very deep, more than a thousand feet in places. The lake is like a drowned canyon encircling a large island, Samosir.

THIS is the country of the Simulungan Bataks. They are said to be more advanced, more interested in education than the Karonese of the region we have come through and the Tobanese who live round the lake we are going to.

They look the same, and the boxy wood-and-sheet-iron houses they live in are without distinction. But they have done first-rate restoration, at a place called Pematang Purba 85 miles from Medan, of the houses that were the primitive palaces of their tribal kings, their *radjas*.

The main radjas' house, with forward-leaning gables finely patterned and bull-horned at the frontal peak, is raised about six feet off the ground on stout wooden piles that have been embellished in black, white and brown with Batak designs. Next to it is a house, also very long and high, where the radjas wives lived (a dozen wives was not uncommon) together, but each having her separate cooking hearth. Inside there is an arrangement of platform beds either side of a middle aisle. The "palace" was lived in by thirteen radjas up to 1945. They never embraced either Christianity or Islam but retained their animistic spirit beliefs.*

The last radja's son went to university and became a lawyer

* Animism (from *anima*, breath or life) is the attribution of soul or spirit to such inanimate objects as stones. It is an aspect of nature worship often interrelated with ancestor worship.

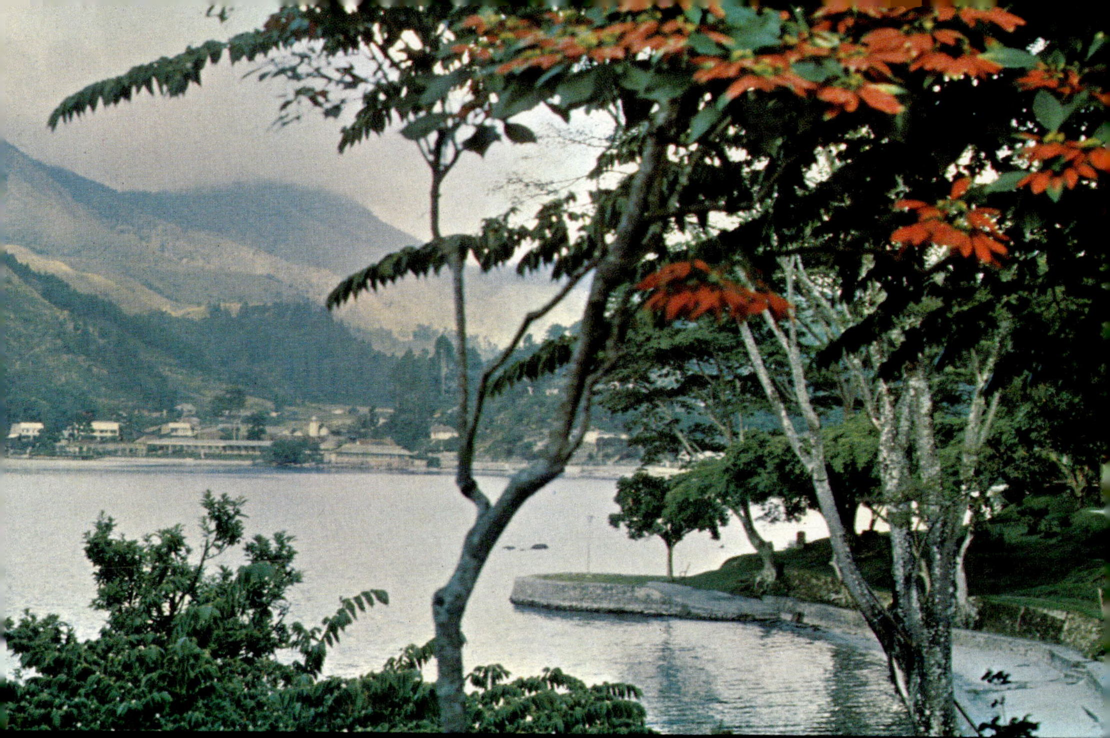

Parapat is the only town on the lake, which has villages on its shores and on a large island. Poinsettia-trees and crotons brighten the grounds of the Parapat Hotel.

NORTH SUMATRA

Author's Ektachromes

"Lake Toba presented itself theatrically . . . as the evening sun rayed down." The lake is large, fifty miles long, mountain-rimmed, and 3,000 feet above sea level.

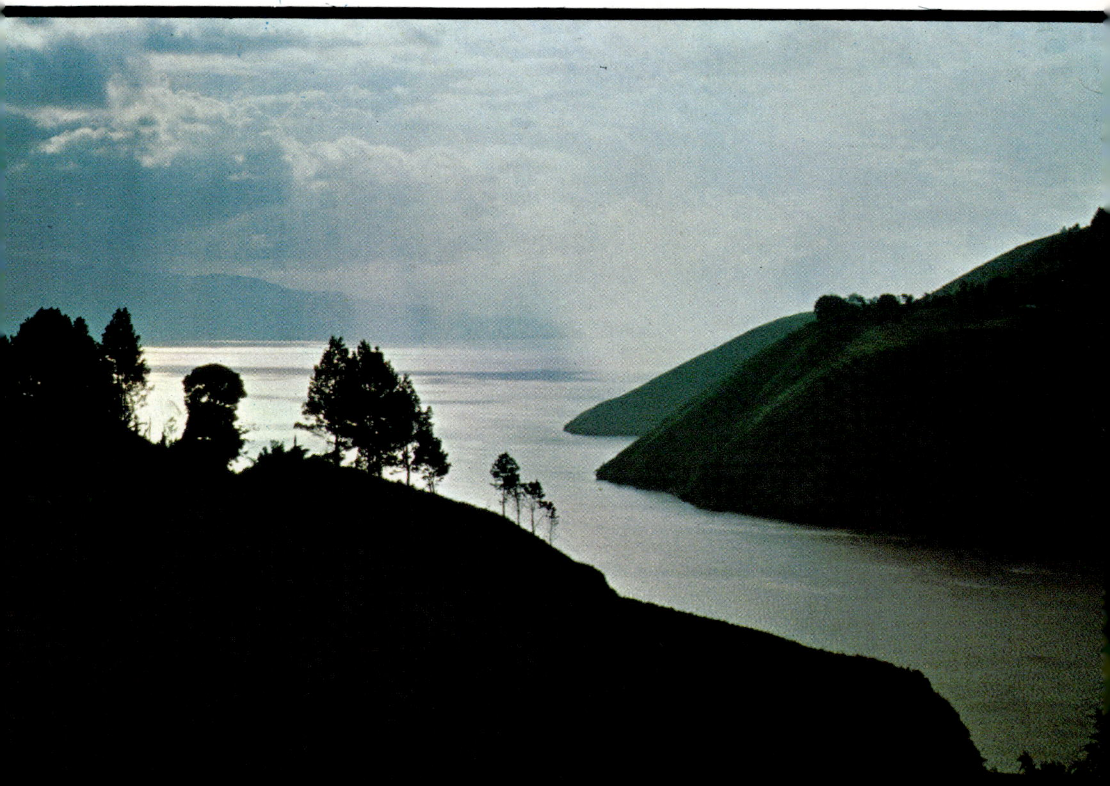

In these long, large "bolon" houses lived the radjas (tribal kings) of the Batak people. Admirably restored, the houses are between Medan and Lake Toba.

NORTH SUMATRA   Author's Ektachromes

Ten of these traditional houses, with roofs curving up to the points of leaning gables, form the village of Djangger, not far from Lake Toba.

Remarkable stone carving, said to date from about 1700, characterizes the sarcophagus of a radja at Tomok on Samosir, the big island in Lake Toba.
NORTH SUMATRA   Author's Ektachromes
Tobanese Batak children of the village of Porsea, not far from the lake, had not seen many tourists, and thought it great fun to be photographed.

SULAWESI (CELEBES)

"Tomorrow country" for tourists is the region of the Toradja
people, who decorate their houses brilliantly and, BELOW, make
wooden effigies of the dead they bury in cliffside tombs.

Ektachromes by courtesy of Garuda Indonesian Airways

and the mayor of Siantar, a town that is the commercial centre of the Batak inland. We turn off this side of Siantar but will stop there on the way back from the lake.

LAKE TOBA presented itself theatrically, all silver-gold and gun-metal as the evening sun rayed down and, striking the water to brilliance, entranced the humped capes of foreshore in deep grey silhouette. Thus, beautifully, the road wound down to Parapat.

This only town on the lake, Parapat, is on a spit of land and is not big enough to be very intrusive. It is wholly a tourist resort, and the tourists who come there are mainly Indonesians and Chinese and Europeans stationed in Indonesia. The Hotel Parapat, well situated right on the lakeshore, was the best place to stay; but some changes needed to be made if Lake Toba was to attract more than the sprinkling of overseas tourists it was getting.

There needed to be, for a start, a dining-room menu in English. It would have Indonesian dishes on it, of course—indeed it should have Sumatran specialities; but it needed to explain that *Nasi Padang* was a spicy rice combination, with chicken, meat, fish or whatever, and *Nasi Soto's* meat and rice came with coconut sauce and chilli ketchup and that *Petjal* with *Galo-gado* was a dish of local vegetables with peanut sauce and spices. As things were, a waiter with only rudimentary English wandered down to your bungalow-type accommodation about an hour before dinner and handed you the menu you couldn't read and wanted to know what you wished to eat that evening. When you couldn't tell him he went away. You got dinner with your guide's aid.

Breakfast was a no-choice meal of fried eggs, canned bully beef, a serving of cheese (a hangover from Dutch days), toast and jam. Mangoes were not available, although they were in season. Not too surprisingly, only two other people were staying at the hotel.

The bungalows were quite adequate considering the moderate tariff, with bathrooms private though rather primitive, and there was plenty of space, with sitting-room and a veranda. But the place had been reconditioned by a Chinese contractor who (and I don't know why the twentieth-century Chinese have such execrable taste) had "picked out" the paintwork in brown, blue, pink, Indian red and a bilious yellow. And, in a garden that had the tropical colours of crotons and poinsettia and hibiscus, the low fence had had its palings painted red-one, yellow-one, blue-one, red again. The only colour any of the paintwork needed to be was white.

There was nothing discoverable to do at night at Parapat while I was there; but when tourist groups came they were regaled with Batak dancing and singing. Bataks had good voices according to Rismono Trio, who had a good voice himself and had won a pop contest in Medan. He rendered a song called *Sing Sing So* which, I gathered, was permanently on top of the Batak hit parade, and was undoubtedly a catchy number. I had not thought that Batak singing groups would use electric guitars, but Rismono said they did.

Next morning we set out by speedboat across the lake to the big and populous island of Samosir that sits in the middle of it. Tomok is the village where you land, and a market was in progress under a big *waringin* (banyan-tree). Women vendors spread their vegetables, spices and other wares in baskets; mothers chatted, babies on their backs in slings; old people squatted and chewed betel nut, which the young disdain. A stall sold finely-woven cloths of distinctive Batak design, which runs to thin stripes, favours red-white-and-black, and has a beautifully dark red that is close to black. The two lengths of cloth I bought also have a thin stripe of chrome yellow. There looked to be a week's weaving in each piece that cost only a few dollars. Subsequently, in Parapat at a stall near the hotel, I got a very fine piece of Batak weaving in a most intricate design, mainly black and white with deep-red touches, and big enough to be a spread for a divan in the flat of a daughter in London, for 3,000 rupiahs, which is roughly six dollars Australian. North Sumatran weaving is surely one of the best textile buys in Indonesia, in Asia, in the world.

Under another big tree called a *hariara* was a marvellous tomb. It was of a *radja* the guide called King Sidabutar and is thought to date from about 1700. One end of the tomb (EKTA-CHROME) is carved with a striking stylized long face with wide eyes, and the back and sides of the head are also arrestingly designed. This head rests on a small seated figure. On the back of this stone sarcophagus is a female figure, probably the radja's principal wife. The adjoining tomb, of later date, has a Christian cross on it. Other tombs, here and elsewhere, take the form of miniaturized Batak *bolon* houses.

Here at Tomok a number of the old Batak big houses put up their curving roofs and slanted gables against the sky, and the shaggy black of the thatch sweeping up to the horns on the point was dramatic against the blue and the puffy white cumulus. But more than half the houses had, instead of the thatch, corrugated-iron—and some of it rusty. It would be better-looking as well as longer lasting if it were painted black or the deep red-black of Batak weaving. But iron that looks awful leaks less than thatch in the raving monsoon's rain. Keep the iron, then, and cover it with thatch for aesthetics sake? Tourism could pay for this. And these spectacular houses need to be preserved, for the villagers are unlikely to build any more of them. The big hardwood timber of the *turi-turi* trees has been just about cut out on the island.

Farther along the lake at the village of Simanindo there were a number of other *bolon* houses. One that was said to be two hundred years old had a fine gable with richly decorative carving. It was the house of Tobanese *radjas*, ten of them evidently, for there were ten sets of water-buffalo horns arranged one above the other inside. The only light that entered—from the small door the entrance ladder leads up to—did little to dispel the interior darkness.

With the aid of a torch I made out a massive radja's bed, shaped like a barge and fashioned from some heavy wood like mahogany. There were some carved small wooden figures, primitive effigies. A curious canopy-like thing made of wood and palm leaf hung from the roof, and under this the *dukun* (witchdoctor) used to perform his magic, and perhaps still did. *Dukuns* were still called in to heal the sick, although Simanindo had a hospital, which was more than Tomok with a population of three thousand had.

One enters the compound where these houses are through

a stone gateway surmounted by a remarkable piece of sculptural decoration. (See drawing on page 85.)

The last house in the group had a regrettable roof that was part corrugated-iron and part tiles, and the facade had been "brightened up" with blue paint and fancywork that looked foreign to the Batak style, and hideous.

We went across to a small island in the lake called Palau Tao: I asked the guide what that name meant and he said, "Lake Island." A brochure said, "On this island a rest-house with complete furnitures and guaranteed cleanness can be found. The rest-house consists of three rooms that can be routed", meaning rented. The building was gaudily Western, but you could drink beer under a small Batak-style pavilion with a fine lake view. There was also a swimming place. The owner of this enterprise was the Medan police chief, who would probably do well out of it eventually. Nobody was staying there; but having morning tea were the other two guests from the Hotel Parapat. Ian Morgan and his wife were appreciating Lake Toba not only for its picturesqueness but for its peacefulness and coolness after the frenetic bustle and humid heat of Djakarta, where they lived.

Both were Australians, and I thought that this big and intelligent man typified the best thing about Australian aid to the underdeveloped countries of Asia. It was, I feel sure, not all the aid that Australia could and should afford. But at least it was provided as a direct gift—not as long-term credits as so much foreign aid was—and much of it was provided in the more-valuable-than-money form of men with expertise. Ian Morgan was in Indonesia to help solve the traffic problem that had Djakarta in knots and was threatening to strangle the city. One of his chief headaches had been the multiplicity of slow-moving *betjaks* tying up the traffic stream. It was his doing that Djakarta·s pedicabs had, instead of names, numbers and colours indicating areas where they could legally operate.

I asked about corruption in the public service and he said it was nothing like it used to be. In Sukarno's time you had to carry a pocket full of notes to scatter on your way through the bureaucratic labyrinth. (To bring in his car he had had to fill in seventeen forms and get them cleared.) But honesty was hardly to be expected, he said, where senior public servants earned as little as fifteen dollars a week. Not that the rich set much of an example. Mercedes cars could be imported with a specially low duty if they were to be used as taxis. So they were wangled in as taxis and promptly became private cars.

Of the massacre of Communists in 1965, Ian Morgan said what Ronald McKie says in his book, *Bali*[8]: many of the killings were motivated by old feuds that found in the anti-Communist pogrom an excuse for giving vent to bloodymindedness normally restrained by law. Of Sukarno he said, "Say what you like, he took all these diverse groups of people and made them into a nation."

OTHER BATAK VILLAGES could be reached by road and one of these, set among ricefields, was called Djangger. Here about ten *bolon* houses faced each other. One had a highly-decorated gable and, inset in the arabesque-like design, were two portraits, a man and a woman. The man was a medical orderly who, during the war against the Japanese, had become a hero to these people.

In this outlying village away from the road, where visitors were few, the Tobanese did not like being photographed—though girls hoeing in the field made quite a game of ducking for cover when I pointed a camera, laughing as they did so. The children didn't mind, but asked for cigarettes. With the adults, their aversion seemed to be a mixture of a feeling that they were being "exploited" by the photographer and the old fear many primitive peoples have that if you have their image you can work magic against them. But these villagers were quite amiable.

A couple of the women brought out cloths they had woven, for sale. One piece, the largest I saw, must have been eight feet long by about four feet wide, and it was a superb piece of weaving almost entirely in black and white. The intricacy of some of the patterning was quite astonishing. The woman asked 6,000 rupiahs for it (about $13 Aust.) and, although bargaining is regular and expected, she was not inclined to take less; nor did I feel that she should, for there looked to be weeks of work in it. Deciding, reluctantly, that I couldn't afford the cloth, I asked the guide what it was used for and he said, "It is for wrapping a dead person." It was a shroud.

At another village, Porsea, along the main road, we asked to see cloth and none was forthcoming. Here the decoration of one house included side panels of scene painting, one a wartime picture of a plane machine-gunning. It was ingenuous, and the traditional designs were so much better.

The Bataks here were about fifty-fifty Christians and Moslems. And one might gather from a brand-new mosque by the roadside that Islam was gaining ground. This was probably to be expected in what had become a Java-oriented Indonesia where Christianity was associated with cast-out colonialism.

The biggest and best-looking mosque in Sumatra is the Mesdjid Raya (Great Mosque) in Medan.

ON THE WAY BACK to Medan from Lake Toba we stopped for lunch at the Siantar Hotel, which is the kind of hotel that is needed at the lake. It served an excellent meal including the *saté* (kebabs) it is famous for. Siantar also has a small, but good, museum strikingly housed in Batak long-house style.

Soon we were running for miles, on this northerly return route, through a Goodyear rubber plantation, the trees either side of the road diagonally striped from the cutting of their bark so that the white latex runs down into the cup attached to each trunk. The tappers come round in the early morning and again at noon. A rubber-tree will begin bearing at about five years and may continue as a producer for twenty-five years before it is cut down for firewood and a new tree planted.

Oil palm plantations are also extensive in this region. The palms are mostly of the dwarf variety that do not grow higher than a man can reach to harvest the clusters of yellow-brown fruit, of which as many as a thousand drupes may grow on one palm, and about half the fruit's weight is palm oil. These palms are not indigenous: the Dutch introduced them from West Africa. Cocoa is also grown here, on its own or between the rows of oil palms, though often there is interplanting of the palms with peanuts.

"Sumatra produces forty per cent of the national income of Indonesia," Rismono said proudly.

Sumatra's greatest contribution, though, came out of the ground in the form of oil that made petroleum. The oil centre was Palembang, which has so little to recommend it to tourists that the Indonesian tourist authorities make no attempt to "sell" Palembang.

It is market day as we come through Tebing Tinggi, fifty miles from Medan, the capital of Deli province and a strong Moslem centre. A bus so crowded that some of the passengers are standing along the rear bumper lurches past the food stalls. A file of women with tall slim baskets balanced on their heads are going to a wedding, Rismono says, and the baskets contain rice they are taking as a present. I tell Rismono that at Western weddings it is an old convention to throw rice at the couple when they emerge from the church. He laughs, and obviously thinks that throwing *nasi*, the staff of Asian life, is a crazier custom than any that Asians have.

The Dirga Surya Hotel in Medan serves not a bad *nasi goreng* but its memorable dish, in my brief experience, is delicious, big-clawed crab. Tea came by the cup, not the pot, and was already sugared unless you directed otherwise. Asking for rice to go with your meat brought a steaming dish of *nasi putih* sufficient to feed a starving family of three.

The Dirga Surya used to be the best hotel in town but now there was the rectilinear modernity of the International Hotel Pardede offering 46 air-conditioned double rooms-with-bath (US $ 17 a day for single occupancy) with "radio, rediffusion, refrigidaire, wall-to-wall carpet and massage" listed as among the amenities. Pardede is a name to conjure with in Sumatra. Mr. T. D. Pardede, a Batak villager's son, owns textile factories, travel services and other hotels. He is reputedly a hard man to work for, but full of the kind of initiative that Sumatra needs if it is ever to get up on the tourist bandwagon.

Mr. Pardede proposed a new Hotel Parapat on Lake Toba, and it was hoped that this would be operating before the end of 1973.

Epilogue

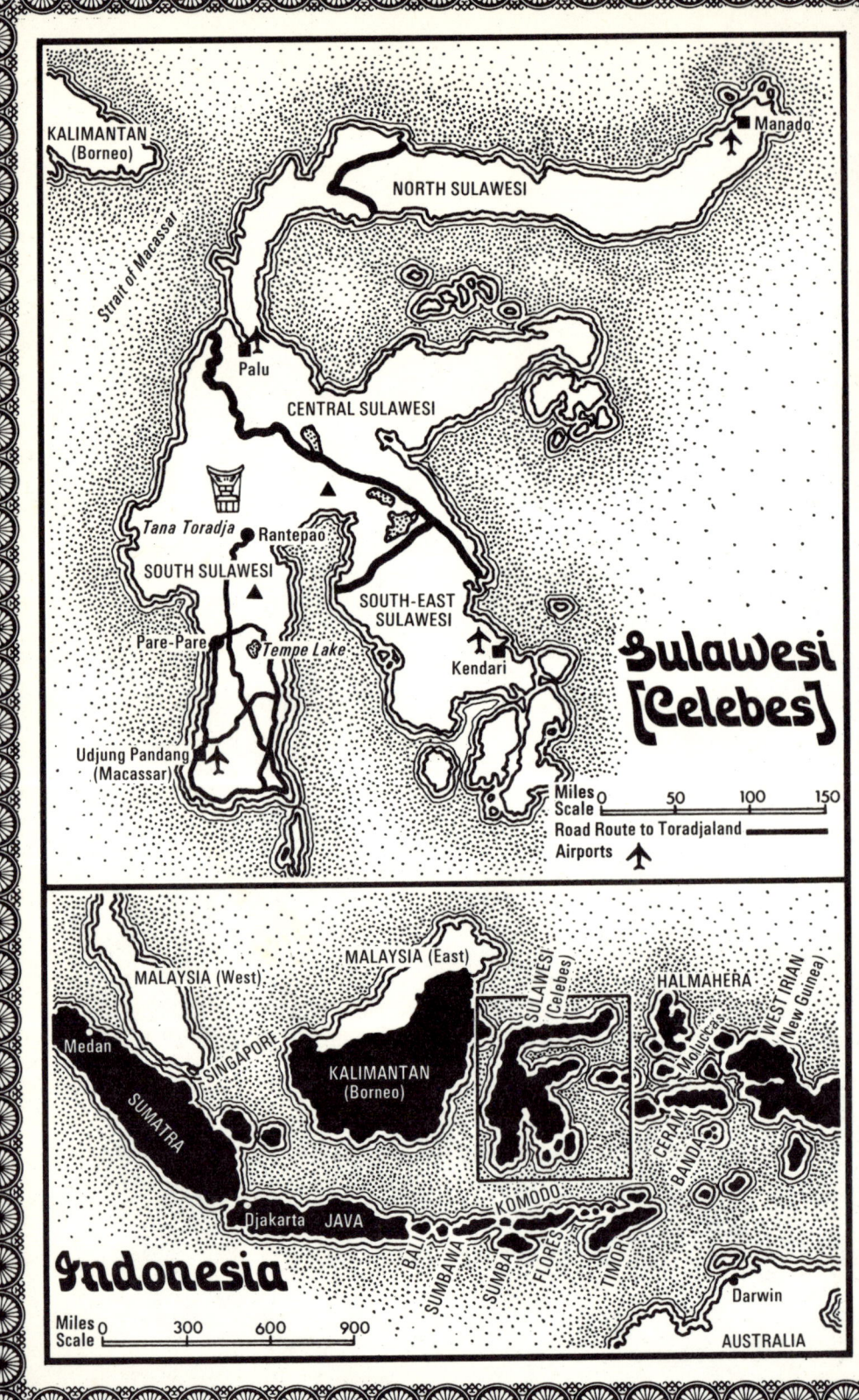

KALIMANTAN
(Borneo)

Strait of Macassar

NORTH SULAWESI

Manado

Palu

CENTRAL SULAWESI

Tana Toradja   Rantepao

SOUTH SULAWESI

SOUTH-EAST
SULAWESI

Pare-Pare   *Tempe Lake*

Kendari

Udjung Pandang
(Macassar)

Sulawesi
[Celebes]

Miles
Scale 0   50   100   150

Road Route to Toradjaland ━━━━
Airports ✈

MALAYSIA (West)   MALAYSIA (East)

Medan

SINGAPORE

SUMATRA

KALIMANTAN
(Borneo)

SULAWESI
(Celebes)

HALMAHERA

Moluccas

WEST IRIAN
(New Guinea)

CERAM

BANDA

Djakarta   JAVA

BALI

SUMBAWA

SUMBA

KOMODO

FLORES

TIMOR

Darwin

Indonesia

Miles
Scale 0   300   600   900

AUSTRALIA

Tomorrow's "beyond" places

INDONESIA is a spread of so many differing islands; yet only Bali, and to a lesser extent Java, are within the average traveller's ken. That is how it is today, but there are places that will change this situation in Indonesian tourism's tomorrow.

Indeed, this rather slim book anticipates putting on some weight of pages in the fairly near future as the *Beyond* part of *Bali and Beyond* extends. With the provision of tourist facilities there, it will take in such places as the Toradja region of Sulawesi (which still appears on many maps as Celebes) and West Sumatra.

These two areas are already on-track to a small number of tourists of the kind not much concerned with comforts and conveniences. Before saying more about them let us just look in the direction of some other places that beckon from a distance and promise to beguile. The Spice Islands, for instance, the Moluccas the Indonesians know as Malaku. If memory serves, Somerset Maugham's novel *The Narrow Corner* was suffused with the nutmeg smell of Banda-Neira the principal port of the ten Banda Islands that are "grouped round a remarkably beautiful inland sea, with splendid marine gardens . . ."[17]

Flores should be, from its name, more tropically flowery than the scanty facts about this island define it as being; but I should still like to see the volcanoes in its visage of mountains eyed with coloured lakes. For the volcano fancier there is no shortage of these in parts of Java I didn't get to. And Flores does not look like coming on-stream touristically before the day after the day after tomorrow.

Off Sumbawa, another of the Lesser Sunda Islands east of Bali, is the isle of Komodo, which is the habitat of *Varanus komodoensis,* largest of lizards, with a thick body that grows to ten feet long. Indonesian tourist literature calls it "the only living dragon", but tours to Komoda don't operate as yet, and for some time we may have to be content with seeing a poor prisoner of the species in some zoo.

An orang-utan ranging free through the jungle is a sight I missed by being several seconds late in rounding a bend in what used to be British North Borneo, and is now Sabah and part of East Malaysia. Nothing seems to be moving, for the tourist, in the jungles of Kalimantan, the Indonesian major part of this large island. And it will be some time yet before the Indonesian half of New Guinea, called Irian Barat, takes off as a tourist destination. But I do feel drawn towards the neighbouring Moluccas.

Nowadays, I realize, the Spice Islands' trade is more in prosaic coconuts than in aromatic cloves; but, "Bird life is profuse and brilliant. . . . Insect life is even richer, and butterflies are remarkably beautiful. Fish and shellfish abound in great variety. . . . Pearl and other shells are traded." I quote not from some gushy leaflet of the travel hucksters but from the factual pages of the *Encyclopaedia Britannica.*[18] The Indonesian tourist literature, if that's the word, says things like: "Cassowaries is found on Seram [Ceram] one of the larger islands, where there is petroleum."

One reason why much of this tourist potential is not likely to develop in a hurry is the lack of expertise in preparing information for the foreign travel trade and its customers about what Indonesia has. The need is to inform and attract, literately and lucidly—and English is a devil of a language for even a well-educated Asian to handle infallibly. So often it comes out sounding awkward and naïve, as when Nitour advertises to travel agents: *Tell your clients and friends to take great adventure to Indonesia's Exotic Tourist Attractions.*

Indonesian tourism is in process of yanking itself up by its bootstraps to host a PATA Conference in 1974, and this should accelerate the process of upgrading services.

By 1975, if not before, the regular tourist should find the kind of facilities he expects, on an adequate but not grand scale, in the two areas mentioned earlier:

(i) *Sulawesi*/TORADJA REGION

The Toradja are one of the half-dozen different peoples of this large island with a peculiar shape that has been described as like an orchid's. Toradjaland or *Tana Toradja* is in mountains about 300 kilometres from South Sulawesi's capital, Macassar—or, as it was renamed in 1971, Udjung Pandang, which means "Land's End" and is a rather ugly mouthful compared with Macassar (which was not one of those Dutch-colonial names Indonesian nationalism detests but is from the native *Mangkasar*).

The Toradja people build picturesque "boat-shaped" houses and rice barns, with long prow-like gables projecting—they have an affinity with the Batak houses of North Sumatra—some of them richly painted, inside and out, with geometrical designs. They entomb their dead in vaults hewn out high in the rock wall of a cliff. Some of these grave-rooms have porches or balconies on which are stood wooden effigies of the dead, fully dressed and about two-thirds life size. (The funeral ceremonies of a Toradja nobleman, in whose honour a dozen water-buffaloes were sacrificed, were described in an article in the June 1972 *National Geographic* magazine.)

Rantepao is the Toradja town that is likely to develop into a tourist resort. Already there is a guest-house called Maria that can take twenty people (who should not expect private baths or other accommodation frills). Thirty kilometres before Rantepao is reached there is the Mess of the District Military Command, and rather more people stay there than at Rantepao, according to Golden Bali Tours who gathered this information for me. GBT also reports that it takes about twelve hours to reach Rantepao by jeep from Macassar. The road north runs through "rugged, fantastically shaped limestone mountains".[18] A stay of two or three days is advisable. With two nights in Macassar (which has reasonably good hotels), a four-night/five-day Macassar-Toradja package tour, including full board, was being offered by tour operators in Macassar/Udjung Pandang in mid-

1972 at around $330 US for one person, $190 US each for two, $145 US for three, $122.50 US for four.

A 200-room modern tourist hotel is to be built at Macassar, which is reputedly picturesque in itself and has scenic attractions in its vicinity. The announcement, "Work has begun on the building, in stages, of a hotel complex in Toradja, South Sulawesi, which when finally completed will have 800 rooms", appeared in a publication of the Indonesian Directorate-General of Tourism in October 1971. My information nine months later was that work on this project had *not* begun.

Plans for a helicopter service between Macassar and Toradja-land were announced. It seemed unlikely that such a service would develop until there were (a) more facilities in Macassar for the type of tourist who can afford excursions by helicopter and (b) more tourist accommodation up in Toradjaland.

Getting to Macassar/Udjung Pandang was no problem if you had the air fare. Garuda Airways and the regional carrier MNA (Marpati Nusantara Airlines) both flew to four points in Sulawesi from Djakarta and Surabaja.

(ii) *West Sumatra*/MENANGKABAU REGION AND NIAS

Not as far up the island of Sumatra as Medan, and on the other side of it, is the port of Padang. You can fly to Padang by Garuda from Djakarta, Medan, or, for that matter, from Singapore (MNA fly there too). Padang can also be reached by bus from Medan. A 1972 report on this direct, twenty-six hour journey across the mountains made it sound ruggedly un-comfortable and a bit hazardous.[19]

Padang itself, I am told, is of no account. The point in flying to it, or getting there by ship, would be to go inland to the Padang Highlands; and also out by ship to the island of Nias. Indonesian tourist information (1971) listed three Padang hotels, one of which actually had baths in ten of its 31 rooms for around $6.

Inland about fifty miles is Bukit Tinggi. It is West Sumatra's chief town, has an "interesting market", and for some travellers its chief charm might be its setting—between two lakes and near a canyon described as magnificent, with walls several hundred feet high.[18] Bukit Tinggi's main interest, it seems to me,

106

could be that it is the capital of the Menangkabau country.

The Menangkabau people "once represented the highest form of Malayan civilization".[18] What makes that assessment, and the people themselves, particularly interesting is that the Menangkabau society was, and still is, matrilineal. Extraordinarily, it retained this woman-oriented character even though it adopted Mohammedanism, a religion whose tenets as to the female role are quite at variance with those of Women's Lib. With the Menangkabau, descent is from the mother and inheritance is down the female line. The women were so business-minded, a 1972 traveller reported,[19] that the Padang Highlands was the one region of Indonesia where the Chinese had never got a commercial footing. "A wife remains after marriage with her kinsfolk on the mother's side, and her husband, having no home of his own, only visits his wife, and resides in his mother's house."[18]

Houses of the Menangkabau are related in style to those of the Batak in North Sumatra and the Toradja of Sulawesi, but their curving rooflines and high-pointed gables appear, from photographs, to be of even better design. Pictures of comely Menangkabau women, rounder of face than most Malays, show them wearing handsome ceremonial hats. The shape of these, curved and peaked, is rather like that of the houses. They are in scarlet trimmed with gold.

Nias is the largest (eighty miles long by thirty) of a chain of islands that lie off the upper west coast of Sumatra. Nias is offshore about a hundred sea miles from the port of Sibolga, north of Padang, from which the island can also be reached by some coastal steamers that call at Padang. Or, having gone to Lake Toba one could continue across the island to Sibolga, which appears to be about the same distance from Parapat as Medan is, not much over a hundred miles. The official *Tourist Map of North Sumatra* does not bother to include a distance scale. The map attached to the 1972 edition of a brochure called *North Sumatra,* has (as the edition I was given did not) two colour photographs of Nias, one of a village of unremarkable houses and the other of a "war" dance that is colourfully costumed. But the text does not tell the traveller anything about the people of Nias except that they exist as a distinct people and the island has a "megalith culture": nothing about what form this culture takes, what there is to see, or how to get there, or whether there is, on the island, anywhere to stay. Sibolga is listed as having one eight-roomed hotel.

Nias is no place I would go specially to Sumatra to see, but if I were again in the area to go to the Padang Highlands, I think I'd go to Nias from Padang. It is an island of rather special interest to the anthropologically minded because of its culture's relative primitivity in this Asian area. Ancestral figures were carved in stone. Menhirs (upright pillars, some apparently phallic) were set up. The pagan Niasese went in for head-hunting and there was human sacrifice at the death of a chief until these practices were stopped by the Dutch. They are, apparently, still pagans. They are said to be good craftsmen in gold, silver and wood.[18]

It may be that some of the pull the place has for me is due to a process of attraction through exasperation. A Sydney travel agency that is supposed to specialize in Indonesian travel knew nothing about the Niasese (nor, for that matter, did it know about the Menangkabau, but thought they were the people who lived round Lake Toba).

However, I have just come upon a reference to Nias's people in a booklet put out by the Indonesian ministry that deals with tourism. It says: "Off the coast of Padang [wrong] is the island Nias, where the 300,000 inhabitants live completely isolated with traditional laws based on stone age culture. It is wellknown for its ritual dances, local architecture and highjumping over stone walls."

That clinches it—probably by telling so little that it leaves to the imagination so much. The next time round in Sumatra I have to go to Nias.

References

The following books and other publications referred to are indicated in the text by small numbers that correspond with the numbers preceding the titles:

1 *Bali,* by Philip Hanson Hiss (Duell, Sloan & Pearce, New York, 1941).
2 *Island of Bali,* by Miguel Covarrubias (Cassell, London, 1937).
3 *Bliss in Bali,* by Jacques Chegaray (Barker, London, 1955).
4 *A Preliminary Analysis of the Inter-action between Balinese and Tourists,* by Philip Frick McKean, B.D., M.A., Asst Professor of Anthropology, Hampshire College, Amherst, Mass., U.S.A. (Bali Museum Directorate, 1971).
5 *Trance in Bali,* by Jane Belo, with preface by Margaret Mead (Columbia University Press, New York/Oxford University Press, London).
6 *Beautiful Bali,* by Sir Robert Blackwood (Hampden Hall, Melbourne, 1970).
7 *Guide to Bali,* published by the Hotel Bali Beach Corporation, 1970.
8 *Bali,* by Ronald McKie (Angus & Robertson, Sydney and London, 1969).
9 Nigel Cameron, writing on Balinese painting in the Thai International Airways magazine, *Sawasdee,* October-November, 1971.

10 E. P. Patanne, writing on "A Rediscovery of Southeast Asia" in the Hong Kong-published magazine *Orientations*, vol. iii, no. i, January 1972.

11 In *History, Science, the Arts and Nature in Sarawak* (1961-62), reprints of chapters by Tom Harrisson from Sarawak's *Annual Report.*

12 D. R. Brothwell, "Upper Pleistocene Human Skull from Niah Caves, Sarawak" in the *Sarawak Museum Journal,* July-December 1960.

13 Prof. Dr. R. M. Sutjipto Wirjosuparto, in *Glimpses of Cultural History of Indonesia* (Indira, Djakarta, 1964).

14 Drs Soediman, *Chandri Laradjonggrang at a Glance*, booklet apparently self-published, Jogjakarta, 1969, with an introduction by the Director of the Archaeological Service, Drs R. Soekomo.

15 *Glimpses of the Borobudur*, by Drs Soediman (Archaeological Foundation, Jogjakarta, 1968).

16 *Your Next Stop INDONESIA,* booklet published by the Directorate-General of Tourism, Djakarta, 1971.

17 *Golden Guide to South and East Asia*, edited by P. H. M. Jones, published by the Far Eastern Economic Review (Paul Flesch, Melbourne, 1971).

18 *Encyclopaedia Britannica,* 1964 edition (William Benton, Chicago, London).

19 Article, "The Road from Padang", by David Jenkins, in the *Sydney Morning Herald,* 17th July, 1972.

Index